SIMPLY
SYNOPSIS

SIMPLY SYNOPSIS

A SIMPLE SYNOPSIS STRATEGY FOR ROMANCE WRITERS

MICHELLE SOMERS

Copyright © 2017 Michelle Somers
Published by Thrasher Publishing

Written by Michelle Somers
Edited by Ruth Kennedy
Cover Design by Lana Pecherczyk

Paperback: 978-0-6480188-3-4
Kindle: 978-0-6480188-4-1
ePub: 978-0-6480188-5-8

A Cataloguing-in-Publication record of this book is
available from the National Library of Australia.

THRASHER
PUBLISHING

To the wonderful writers I've met through Melbourne Romance Writers Guild and Romance Writers of Australia.

Without your love, support and guidance, this book would never have been born.

Table of Contents

PRAISE FOR *SIMPLY SYNOPSIS*

'Michelle Somers demystifies one of the toughest things an author will ever have to write. *Simply Synopsis* is a worthy investment in your career and needs pride of place on your writing craft shelf.'

STEFANIE LONDON, USA Today Bestselling Author

'Loved Michelle Somers's *Simply Synopsis*—it's easy to read and simple to follow!'

RACHAEL JOHNS, International Bestselling Author

'In this simple, example-rich guide, Michelle Somers delivers not only the steps to constructing a pain-free synopsis, but a whole novel-writing course in digest form.'

VALERIE PARV AM, International Bestselling Author

'*Simply Synopsis* takes the mystery and misery out of writing a synopsis. No writer should be without it.'

ALLI SINCLAIR, Ausrom Book of the Year 2014

'*Simply Synopsis* is a useful and concise guide to tackling the dreaded synopsis. This book is an author's lifesaver!'

KYLIE GRIFFIN, National Bestselling Author

'For any author who has ever struggled to write a synopsis, this is a must-have resource, and one that will be pulled off the shelf again and again to refresh and perfect one's craft.'

ANNA CAMPBELL, Bestselling Author of the *Dashing Widows* series

A WORD FROM THE AUTHOR

My writing journey has been one of blessings – angels in the form of mentors flitting into my life, imparting their knowledge and experience, helping mold me into the writer I am today.

The *Simply Writing Series* is a culmination of the skills I've gained and my scientific mind processing and putting them into practice. I hope the logical progression of my thoughts and the resulting strategies assist writers the world over in building on the craft knowledge they have, culminating in a story or stories that rock the world. And hopefully, somewhere in all this, I will be able to demystify the mystifying and transform writing into an easier and less stressful endeavor.

With that said, let's get started!

GLOSSARY OF TERMS

Antagonist – a character who actively opposes the protagonist in a story; adversary or nemesis of the central character.

Black moment – the point in a story when all seems lost and it seems impossible that the central characters will find their happy ever after. This immediately precedes the climax.

Blurb – a short description of a book, film or other product written for promotional purposes (*Oxford Dictionary*).

Central characters – the primary characters driving your story. In a romance, these are your love interests; in a classic romance, this is your hero and heroine.

Central theme – what happens to your characters as a result of your plot. *See* premise.

Character – a person in a novel, play or film.

Character arc – the inner journey of a character over the course of a story.

Climax – a plot's highest point of tension and drama. Immediately follows the black moment and marks the instant the central characters face the conflict head-on and start to solve it.

Conclusion – the end of a story where all plotlines are tied up and all conflicts are resolved.

Conflict – a physical barrier (external conflict) or psychological belief or fear (internal conflict) obstructing a character from reaching their goal.

Dystopian – relating to a fictional society or world in which everything is unpleasant or bad.

Elevator pitch – a succinct and persuasive sales spiel.

External conflict – a character's struggle against outside forces or events.

GMC – 'Goal, Motivation, Conflict' in relation to the characters in a story.

Goal – what the character wants or strives for in the story. This can be external (a tangible item) or internal (their emotional state).

Happy ever after (HEA) – the conclusion of a romance where the central characters resolve all conflicts and embark on a contented and happy life together.

Happy for now (HFN) – a moment where the central characters are happy and content without reason or conflict to keep them apart. This doesn't speak to the future so much as that one moment in time.

Heart's talk – a candid, intimate, personal conversation. Often emotion-rich, where secrets and/or feelings are revealed, bringing two or more characters closer together.

High concept – a simple, easily communicable idea in relation to a story and its premise.

Higher stakes – a character's higher or more personal interest in an outcome, i.e., what a character stands to gain or lose if the plot doesn't go their way.

Hook – a sentence that nabs the audience's interest and builds their expectations. In this guide the hook relates to the first sentence in the orienting paragraph of a synopsis.

Inciting incident – an incident early in a story that jolts the central character out of their normal life and into the adventure that is your plot. In romance, this tends to be linked in some way to the meet cute.

Internal conflict – a character's internal struggle with their emotions or insecurities.

Logline – usually three or four sentences long, a logline summarizes the plot and the central characters' GMCs, and it give a sense of higher stakes.

Major plot point – a significant event that impacts the direction of the storyline and/or impacts the central characters' growth and/or relationship arc. Used interchangeably with 'major turning point'.

Major turning point – *see* major plot point.

Motivation – the drive behind a character's desire to achieve their goal.

No turning back now – equivalent to the 'point of no return' in a plot, where a character is fully committed to their journey and turning back will result in dire consequences. In romance this can encompass turning points such as sparks of trust, sharing, intimacy and making love for the first time.

Opportunity knocks – plot point where opportunity arises that makes movement toward a character's goal possible.

Pacing – the speed at which your story moves through time. A fast-paced story is action-filled and gripping; a slow-paced story can be laborious and cumbersome to read.

Pantser – a writer who doesn't plot, but writes organically, by 'the seat of their pants'.

Plot – the storyline of your story; a sequence of events arranged in such a way as to make a story.

Plot point – a story event.

Plot hole – a gap or hole in a storyline that disrupts the flow and logic of the plot. It constitutes an omission of critical information and results in a nonsensical story or plot point.

Plot twist – an unexpected development in a story.

Plotter – a writer who plots each step in their story before beginning to write.

Plantser – a writer whose writing process includes elements of both plotting and pantsing.

Point of difference – what sets a story and/or characters apart from others in the same genre.

Point of no return – *see* no turning back now.

Premise – this equates to the central theme of your story. It is high concept, taking a series of complex plotlines and consolidating them into one simple idea that immediately attracts interest, and that can be quickly and easily communicated.

Protagonist – the main character, around whom the action or story revolves.

Query – an introduction or covering letter for a book submission to an agent, editor, film producer, etc.

Resolution – point in the story where the central characters risk everything to overcome the obstacles and/or conflicts to achieve their final goal.

Romance – a genre of fiction encompassing a romantic theme with a happy ending.

Romantic elements – romance is present but not the main theme of the plot.

Scener – a writer who writes their story based on a series of scenes rather than plot points.

Secondary characters – supporting characters to the main story; can complement the central characters and help move the plot forward in some way.

Secondary plot – a side story that supports or highlights the main plot.

Spoiler – a statement that divulges a surprise, such as a plot twist, the climax and/or ending of a story.

Subgenre – a subdivision of a genre. Examples of subgenre in romance are suspense, comedy, futuristic and historical.

Subplot – *see* secondary plot.

Synopsis – a summary that breaks down a story's central plot, introducing the central characters in a concise but interesting way.

Tagline – a one-sentence summary of no more than ten words that is high concept and defines the central theme of a story.

Turning point – a point in the plot where a significant change in a situation occurs.

World-building – the process of constructing entirely new, imaginary species, worlds and/or universes for the purposes of fictional storytelling.

INTRODUCTION
THE NECESSARY EVIL

The synopsis. Why do we do it? Why waste precious time, brain power and energy over something more stressful than writing an entire novel – an entire series, even? Surely there are better ways to spend our time; more productive, like writing that next best seller; or more fun, like curling up with a favorite novel and cheap – or not so cheap – glass of wine.

So, why the wily synopsis?

Because it's near impossible to gain a publishing contract without one. Avoidance won't change this. Believe me, I've tried. So, what alternative do we have but to condense our masterpiece of 80,000-plus-words into a few pages?

Easy, right? *Wrong!*

How do we craft a synopsis using oh, so few words, yet still make it as engaging and captivating as our entire story without losing its essence? Where do we even start? Questions I'll warrant aren't unfamiliar to you, given you've purchased this book.

First, let's understand why it's important to condense our plot and pare it back to its most basic elements.

What is a synopsis?

A synopsis is a summary that breaks down your story's central plot, introducing the central characters in a concise but interesting way. Note the words 'central plot', 'central characters' and 'concise'. Bear these in mind as we'll revisit them later.

Also, note that I added the words 'interesting way' into my definition. A synopsis is not a list of mechanical, matter-of-fact instructions like those you'd find in a manual. While a synopsis outlines the plot of your story, it shouldn't focus on plot alone. Just as your story has nuance and texture, so should your synopsis.

The best way to achieve this is to include emotions. Yes, we need to know what happens in the story, but we also need to know how these events affect the central characters. Just as emotions add depth to your story, so too will they add depth to your synopsis. Don't underestimate their power or their importance here. If the purpose of a synopsis is to hook your reader, what better way to do this than to make them empathize with your characters by showing how they feel?

What's the purpose of a synopsis?

There are multiple benefits to creating a well-crafted synopsis, but I'm going to point out the six I view as most important:

1. Ensures all vital elements are present in your story.
2. Highlights deficiencies in your characterization and GMC (goal, motivation and conflict).
3. Pinpoints the central theme of your story.
4. Pinpoints pacing problems.
5. Pinpoints plot holes or inconsistencies.
6. Sells your book to an editor or agent or screen director.

Of course, most of you will recognize the last point and wonder why I haven't made it the first. Yes, submitting and selling your work for publication is huge. And yes, these days most agents and publishers will request a synopsis as part of their submission package. The length may vary, but the essence is still the same: outline the major plot points and give a brief rundown of your main characters.

But what if, even after your book is done, dusted and ready to submit, you're still not clear on your characters, their goals, their motivation and – heaven forbid – their conflict? What if you're missing some of the vital plot points that make a story unputdownable? What if you have plot holes or pacing problems? Using the *Simply Synopsis* step-by-step process, you will identify these problems before you submit and you will gain the opportunity to 'fix' any holes or deficiencies before sending your baby out into the big blue yonder.

So, now that I've sold you on the idea of a synopsis, let's see if we can make the process of creating it less cumbersome, less stressful and even – dare I say it? – more enjoyable.

Let's take a look at the *Simply Synopsis* system, step-by-step.

CHAPTER 1
SIMPLY SYNOPSIS OVERVIEW

Many ideas and strategies exist on how best to build a synopsis; mine is but one. The *Simply Synopsis* method has been invaluable in helping me enter, place and win in competitions. And it helped me secure a publishing contract with Penguin Random House for my debut novel, *Lethal in Love*. I hope it will help you gain the same success.

Simply Synopsis structure

The *Simply Synopsis* structure comprises of four parts:

1. Orientation
2. Major turning points
3. Resolution
4. Conclusion

In the following chapters, we'll explore each of these steps in depth, focusing on how to build a rock-solid synopsis – structure, composition and formulation – as well as one of the many perplexing decisions: what information to include and what information to safely leave out. This includes a comprehensive look at how to handle backstory.

Synopsis lengths vary subject to submission guidelines. Primarily in this book, we'll cover the longer synopses (2–5 pages) before visiting how to carve back on content to create medium (one page/600 words), mini (300 words) and mini-mini (100 words) synopses.

But first, one point we must clarify before we move on . . .

Spoilers and endings

Should we include spoilers and endings in a synopsis? Absolutely. This is not a blurb where unanswered questions are fundamental in creating suspense to entice readers to buy your book. You are not using your synopsis to sell your book to your readership. Your synopsis is your selling tool to let agents or editors know you understand the qualities of a riveting story and riveting storytelling.

That said, *a synopsis should not finish without answering all the questions it raises*.

Notice I don't say 'all the questions raised in the story'. This was deliberate. A synopsis is not the place to include ALL the questions or turning points in your story. You should include only the major turning points. And even then, you will be constrained by the prescribed length of your synopsis, which will in turn determine how many of these major turning points you include and how deep you delve into each one.

Don't leave plot threads untied or the editor hanging at the end of your synopsis. This is not clever – it's just annoying. Include spoilers and identify red herrings. In the case of a whodunnit mystery, make sure at the end we know 'whodunnit'. Crimes should be solved. Conflicts resolved. Romances tied up satisfactorily. If something's broken, fix it; if something's lost, make sure it's found. The editor or agent wants to know how you end your story – they want to know if you have the skills and ability to end a story well – and they will get frustrated if you don't tell them. Leave the suspense and cliffhangers for your blurb and other marketing tools – things you'll need *after* you've won that anticipated publishing contract.

So, now that misconception is out of the way, let's get started.

CHAPTER 2
ORIENTATION

I refer to the critical opening paragraphs of the synopsis as the 'orientation'. These paragraphs are vital for orienting the reader into your story and making them want to read on.

The orientation of your synopsis must cover several key points. Where and when is the story set? Who is it about? What is the central idea of the story? What is the tone of the story? What is the genre?

There are four critical components that will help you answer these questions and more in your opening paragraphs:

1. The hook
2. World-building
3. Central theme
4. Central characters

I. THE HOOK
What is a hook?

Your hook is the first line of your synopsis.

When most of us think of a hook, we think of a fish, of catching then reeling it in before it has a chance to escape. This is the idea behind the hook in your synopsis.

As the first sentence, your hook is like the set-up to a joke: it nabs your audience's interest and builds their expectations, clearly signaling that something interesting is about to take place. It's that whole 'a funny thing happened to me on the way here today . . .' type scenario. It's a statement at the beginning of your synopsis that says,

'Hey, this is a story you won't want to miss' and 'Don't go anywhere, there's a punch-line coming.'

A hook is *short*, *sharp* and *suspenseful*.

Just one sentence – that's all you need – a concept, to give a sense of your main character's state of mind or the wider, central theme of your story. Don't forget, your story already has a hook – or it should have! – so this is just a matter of sifting the wonderful tributary that is your manuscript to get to the gold. And once the gold has been extracted, like any prized possession, it takes pride of place on your metaphorical mantelpiece, for all and sundry to admire.

If you're struggling to find a hook in your manuscript, then it is likely your reader will too. At this stage, it will pay to go back to the drawing board and work out the central theme of your story. You'll find more on central themes in Chapter 2: Central themes.

It's better to discover your story needs work at this point, when you have the opportunity to amend the problem. Finding out after submission can lead to a lost opportunity – many agents and publishers won't revisit an already rejected manuscript, no matter how much work you've put into revising and reworking it again.

So, all that said, what is the purpose of a hook?

What should a good hook do?

- » Identify the purpose of your writing
- » Lead the reader to ask a question
- » Connect the reader to one or more characters
- » Provide a tantalizing taste of the story
- » Hint at the setting
- » Entice the reader to read on.

Identify the purpose of your story

As the first sentence of your synopsis, the hook wields a wealth of power in highlighting the purpose of your story. When identifying your purpose, ask yourself these two questions:

1. How do I want my audience to feel?
2. What do I want my audience to take away?

Why ask these questions? Because a great hook will lead the reader where you want them to go. It will lead them to think what you want them to think and feel what you want them to feel. A great hook will control the way the reader reads and views what you're about to do or show them next.

Don't underestimate the power of a great hook. Set the tone, grab your audience and whatever you do, don't let them go. Get this first part of your synopsis right and your reader will have no choice but to read on.

Types of hooks

1. Vivid setting description

Setting the scene is an important function of the orienting paragraphs. If you can create a hook that does this, while throwing a dash of world-building into the mix, not only have you offered a wealth of information with an economy of words, but you've enticed the reader into your setting and intrigued them into reading on.

Example

Beneath the hellish fires of 1666 London lies an evil far worse than any devil imaginable.

Not only does this hook give the reader a sense of time and place, but with its language it evokes emotion – trepidation – and gives a hint at some great evil at play. Don't know about you, but I'd definitely read on.

2. Mysterious situation

The hook provides great opportunity to create mystery and tension, to lead the reader into asking questions all the while forcing them to read on because they just *have to* discover the answers.

Example

Lethal in Love (Michelle Somers)

JAYDA THOMASZ has a past so deeply guarded, even she doesn't know it exists.

What is this deep, dark secret in Jayda's past? How is it possible that she doesn't know it exists? These questions, and more, immediately spring to mind when reading this hook. What do you think? Has it grabbed your interest? Could you stop reading here or has this statement hooked you into reading on?

3. A fact

Not only can this type of hook give an indication of your story's central theme, but it has the potential to be chilling, shocking or surprising, once again enticing your audience to continue reading to find out where your story is headed.

Example

90% of assault victims know the perpetrator.

For ASHLEY SCOTT, this is more than a statistic – it's a terrifying reality that suggests her sister's killer is close. Someone she knows. Perhaps even someone she loves.

Pretty riveting, right?

4. A quote (or misquote)

These hooks, especially the misquotes, can be a lot of fun. It's a matter of taking some statement, quote or cliché and turning it into something unique. Make it your own, and make it work for you in the context of your story.

Example

Love is a drug.

And for librarian ANNIE SIMMONS—twice burned and two fiancés down—love is one high she'll never succumb to again. That is, until sexy model RORY WEST crosses her path.

5. Plot twist

This type of hook can hint at the central theme and drag your reader straight into the heart of your story.

Examples

1. For the lost souls of Vandaar, death is only the beginning.

2. Sometimes losing is the only way to win.

3. Love often calls when the doorbell's defunct.

Anna Campbell provides a perfect example of a plot twist hook in her fabulous *Seven Nights in a Rogue's Bed*:

When cataloguing the family library, SIDONIE FORSYTHE discovers proof that her vile brother-in-law WILLIAM MERRICK has no right to the title Viscount Holbrooke.

What a twist! Anna has cleverly left the reader questioning what Sidonie will do with this information, and to what lengths her brother-in-law will go to keep it secret. And true to Anna's writing style, it's riveting reading.

6. A question

This is not the ideal way to open a synopsis. For many agents or editors, questions in a synopsis are pet hates. However, if you do decide to open this way, make sure your question is answered before your concluding paragraph.

As I mentioned earlier, a synopsis should not end leaving the reader with questions. Whether your synopsis forms part of a competition entry or a submission to a potential editor/agent, you want to demonstrate your skill in tailoring a great story. That includes ensuring all your loose story threads are skillfully tied up, leaving the reader happy and satisfied.

Examples

1. Would life after death be so terrible?

2. Who said there was only one man for each woman?

In her novel *Claiming the Courtesan*, Anna Campbell cleverly demonstrates the effective use of questions in a synopsis:

> *Is love powerful enough to redeem a man damned by hatred, lust and his thirst for revenge? Can London's most notorious woman reawaken the virgin heart she cast away when she sold her body at the age of fifteen?*

Consider the power of these two questions. The language, the world-building, the tone. Can a hook get any stronger? Anna has cleverly dropped the reader straight into the 1800s with these first two sentences, and she's made sure they won't want to come out until they discover the answers to each question.

Giving a hook context

Once you've written your fabulous hook, the next step is putting it into context. There's no point in crafting a wonderful piece of prose if the reader has no idea how it relates back to your story. And the synopsis should be all about your story. Much as you want to *wow* your reader with your writing prowess, you must do it with an economy of words. Your hook must tie in somehow with either your plot or your characters, and you'll need to show the reader how.

With one short sentence, join hook and story together:

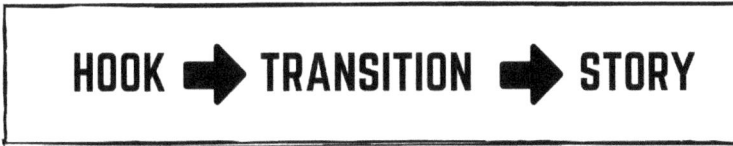

HOOK ➡ TRANSITION ➡ STORY

Let's take a look at some examples.

Example 1

Lucy's Love Lessons (Michelle Somers)

Lies never stay secret forever. A lesson CEO LUCY CONNOR's ex-husband taught her for two long years until she walked out, leaving him and any idea of love behind. So when architect JACK SMITH proposes more than a building contract, she ignores the call of her heart and resolves to share nothing more than a work relationship.

Ooh, what does this tell us? We have an idea of the central theme of the story: *lies never stay secret forever.* And we've gained insight into Lucy's state of mind as the story starts: she's jaded and doesn't believe in love. This is simply delicious, a recipe for disaster when we introduce her hero, Jack Smith, a man searching for a relationship. Conflict galore! So important in a romance, and something we'll delve deeper into later.

If we break this paragraph down and analyze the make-up of this hook, this is what we find:

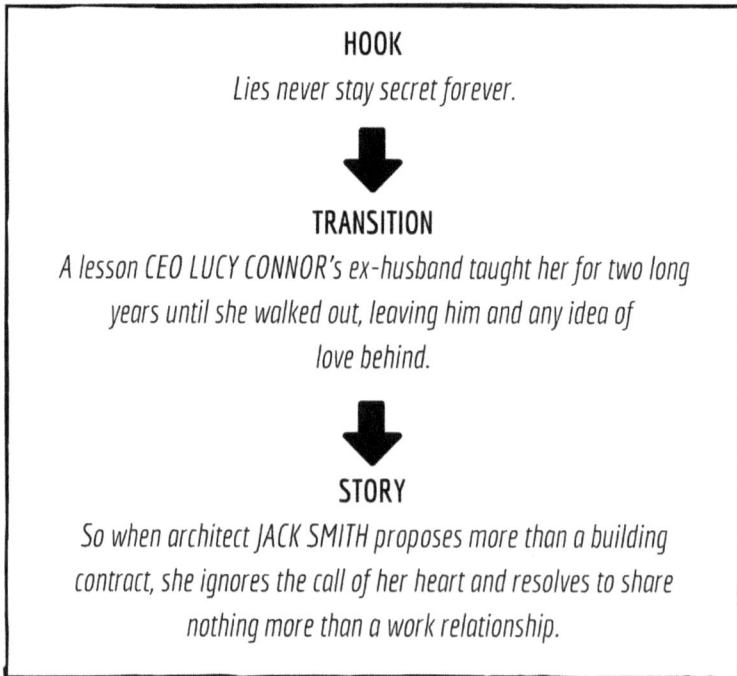

HOOK

Lies never stay secret forever.

⬇

TRANSITION

A lesson CEO LUCY CONNOR's ex-husband taught her for two long years until she walked out, leaving him and any idea of love behind.

⬇

STORY

So when architect JACK SMITH proposes more than a building contract, she ignores the call of her heart and resolves to share nothing more than a work relationship.

Example 2

Games of Seduction (Michelle Somers)

Psychologist MARCY KEENES has had it with heartache. Twenty five, not one to take relationships casually, she's fresh out of an entanglement with her cheating boss and looking for love without lies. No more racing hearts and mind-melting attraction, the man to share her future and win her love will be solid, serious and secure.

Erotic photographer ROBBIE CURTIS is just the one to ease Marcy out of her funk. If only his deserting mother and cheating ex-fiancé hadn't left him jaded and distrustful of women, and more focused on managing his career than matrimony. A little casual seduction, however, is not out of the question.

HOOK
Psychologist MARCY KEENES has had it with heartache.

⬇

TRANSITION
Twenty five, not one to take relationships casually, she's fresh out of an entanglement with her cheating boss . . .

⬇

STORY
. . . and looking for love without lies.
No more racing hearts and mind-melting attraction, the man to share her future and win her love will be solid, serious and secure.

Example 3

The Finn Factor (Rachel Bailey)—New Adult Romance

Rachel has provided me with her back-cover blurb – a fantastic hooking paragraph that could just as easily form part of a synopsis.

Sometimes all a girl needs is a little practice . . .

It's been twelve months, three days and eleven hours since accounting student SCARLETT LOGAN made it past a second date. Clearly someone needs to teach her how to kiss properly. Like, say, her best friend and roomie, FINN MACKENZIE. He's safe, he's convenient, and yeah, maybe just a little gorgeous.

Look how adeptly the hook relates back to the story. Scarlett's dilemma is summed up beautifully, and I'm already a little in love with Finn. This short, sharp paragraph is conflict central, and intriguing enough to have made me go out and buy the book!

HOOK

Sometimes all a girl needs is a little practice . . .

⬇

TRANSITION

It's been twelve months, three days and eleven hours since accounting student SCARLETT LOGAN made it past a second date.

⬇

STORY

Clearly someone needs to teach her how to kiss properly. Like, say, her best friend and roomie, FINN MACKENZIE. He's safe, he's convenient, and yeah, maybe just a little gorgeous.

See how these three examples flow, how they make sense of the hook and meld it seamlessly to the body of the synopsis. Without a transition, these clever, high-concept sentences would float aimlessly above your synopsis.

Do your hook justice. Connect it to your story. Give it context. Give it purpose. Hook your reader and let the transition reel them right on in.

Your turn . . .

Here's a hook – see what you can do using the hook-transition-story method.

> *Be careful what you wish for, it might not be what you really want.*

How many possibilities can you create? What story can you make out of this and how can you link or transition between the hook and story?

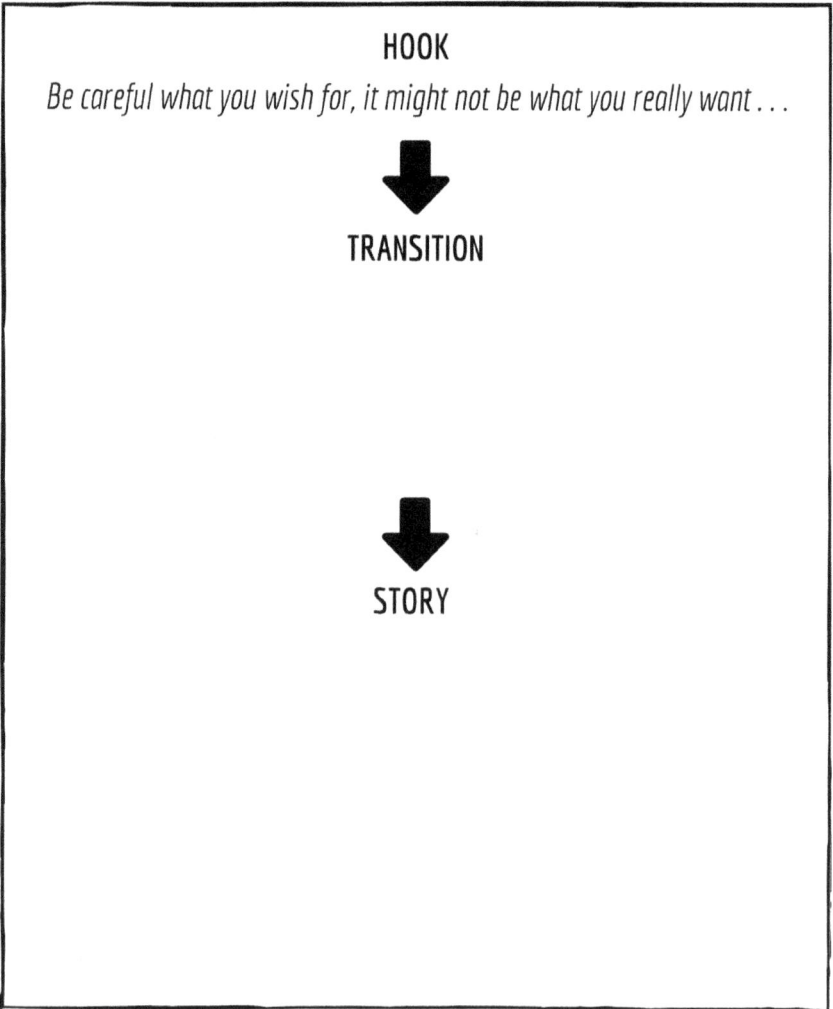

HOOK

Be careful what you wish for, it might not be what you really want . . .

⬇

TRANSITION

⬇

STORY

Now see if you can create a hook using one or more of the six types of hooks, and link it to a story using a transitional statement.

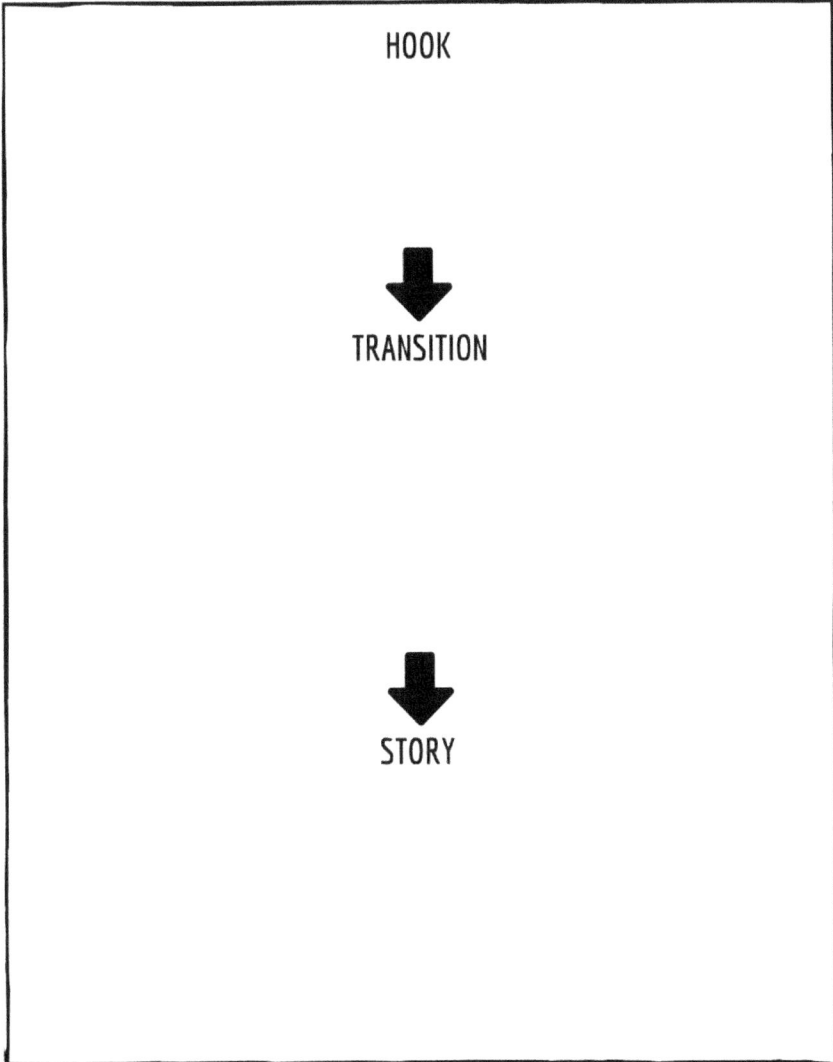

HOOK

⬇

TRANSITION

⬇

STORY

2. WORLD-BUILDING

World-building is the process of constructing entirely new, imaginary species, worlds and/or universes for the purposes of fictional storytelling. If your story takes place in a world or time that's not our own, it's important to set the scene immediately. The sooner you entice the reader into your world, the sooner they'll immerse themselves into your story and won't want to come out.

Saying that, we're not looking for an encyclopedia entry on where your story is set. This is a synopsis, a brief summary of your story – the keyword being 'brief'. Include only enough to orient the reader without bogging them down in a quagmire of detail.

If your story is set in the past or the future, it's important to include the year. If it's another world or planet, hint at the one factor that is central to the theme or plot, the one factor that sets that world or planet apart from the familiar.

Point of difference

What sets your story apart from others in your genre? What sets your characters apart from other such characters? Find this point of difference, and not only will this serve as a hook, but it'll give the reader a sense of the world you've created and intrigue them enough to want to know more. That means they'll just 'have to' read your book! Given that the 'reader' is more-than-likely an editor or agent, and your objective is to snag both their interest and a contract, this is exactly what you want your synopsis to do.

So, how can we show this 'point of difference'? *Find a word or two that define your world and/or your characters.*

Example
Birthright – Beacon 1 (Valerie Parv AM)

Multi-published, award-winning author Valerie Parv AM has a great example of this in her Beacon series. But before I share it, let's take a look at the blurb of the first book in the series, *Birthright*, to provide a little background about this story:

> *Adam Desai is a self-made man. From humble and mysterious origins he has built a career as the director of a prestigious space center. He is also a man who knows right from wrong, and something about the impending launch of the shuttle Arrafin seems very wrong.*
>
> *Deputy Governor Shana Akers is used to handling high-stakes situations. But can she believe Adam's suspicions? The launch is worth millions to the local area, and she knows she's not always the most level-headed when it comes to Adam.*

Now, Valerie's comments:

> *'It took a long time for me to see that my Beacons fit the term "superheroes". They don't wear tights or capes, but each has a unique superpower that is crucial to how each of the Beacon stories unfolds.'*

Perfect! Now all you need to do is identify that same uniqueness in your story and/or characters and present it in a way that captivates the reader.

Example
Listener Garrett can hear anything he wants from across a room to across a universe.

This is brilliant! Not only does this line serve as a hook, but it also gives a sense of the world you're about to enter when you pick up one of Valerie's Beacon books.

Weave world-building into character descriptions and plot

This is crucial not only for your synopsis, but for your manuscript as well. It's the old, 'show, don't tell' dogma. Rather than dropping paragraph-upon-paragraph of world and character information into your synopsis, thread the important details into your plot points.

When looking to build your synopsis, there are a couple of great examples of this in Suzanne Collins' *The Hunger Games*.

Spoiler alert for those who haven't read the first book or seen the movie.

The Hunger Games is a dystopian story set in Panem, a country made up of the wealthy Capitol and twelve poverty-stricken districts. Every year two children per district are selected to participate in a compulsory death contest called 'The Hunger Games'.

In the Hunger Games' arena where contestant, or 'tribute', Katniss Everdeen fights for her life, we don't need to know that the game controllers can manipulate weather and conditions under its dome until a plot point occurs that shows us.

There's an example early in the competition when Katniss strays too close to the outer regions of the arena. The controllers create a forest fire to lure her further into the center, and as a consequence she sustains burns that lead to another important revelation about the game: each tribute can gain sponsors who will send gifts into the arena to help their fight. We discover this when sponsors send Katniss the burn cream that probably saves her life.

Then there are facts in the book that wouldn't need to be included in the synopsis at all. For example, 'trackerjackers'. These are genetically engineered wasps. Do we need to know this in our synopsis? No. In a longer synopsis, we may, however, need to know that these wasps are highly venomous, can cause powerful hallucinations and, in some cases, even death. And when should we discover this fact? When Glimmer, another tribute, is stung so many times that she succumbs to the venom and dies.

In both book and movie, competition updates occur throughout the story via the Hunger Games TV chat show. Do we need to see these in the synopsis? No. Nothing is lost by leaving these scenes out.

Do we need mentions of secondary characters such as Effie who escorts Peeta and Katniss to the Capitol or Cinna, Katniss's stylist? No. Definitely not by name, and neither of these characters – as fascinating and flamboyant as they are – were central to any of the major turning points. Even former winner of the games, Haymitch, would receive barely a mention. When we focus on the romance portion of this story, we focus on Katniss and Peeta. Any other characters are incidental.

KISS–Keep It Simple Stupid

Keep things simple, both in the synopsis and the manuscript – a valuable point that shouldn't be limited to the world-building portions of either. Any complexities in your story – in your world-building or the greater plot – should be pared back and simplified in your synopsis. Leave all the background and detail for your manuscript.

As an example, I asked Valerie to provide insight on how she dealt with the uniqueness of her characters in her Beacons' series. Here's what she had to say:

> '*I tried resolving the Beacons' powers in physiological terms but it was impossible. Instead, I decided to adopt the old sci-fi tradition of "hand wavium" – just waving a hand and saying "this is the power they have". The more you try to explain, the more holes you leave for critics to unravel. I also recommend using shorthand for your world-building, saving the details for the manuscript itself. For example, I used the shorthand "an alien warship" instead of detailing appearance, model and other features of the vehicle. I also refer to "a pair of mysterious visitors". There was no need to go into specifics of who and what they were, outside of their function in terms of driving the plot.*'

It's the whole 'less is more' scenario. Sometimes explanations only serve to confuse the reader. And in a synopsis situation, when you need the reader on your side – when you need them to love the concept of your story, to want to read the whole book and decide it is worth investing in – KISS is often the best and only way to go.

Brevity

Another factor that should not be limited to the world-building portion of your synopsis is brevity. This goes hand in hand with KISS – keep it simple, keep it brief, and write a pacier, more riveting piece of fiction.

While it's important to give your reader a feel for the world in which your novel is set, it's not necessary to include an entire Encyclopedia entry. You don't need to explain the whys and wherefores. Pare back your descriptions, use an economy of words and whip your reader away on a whirlwind tour. In-depth specifics are for your manuscript, not your synopsis.

Example

Award-winning futuristic and fantasy author Kylie Griffin has a great example of how brevity can hook and provide more than enough information to orientate the reader.

Vengeance Born—#1 Light Blade series (Kylie Griffin)

There is no mercy in the demon realm. No escape. In this place of desperation and conflict, anyone who is not pure bred is virtually powerless. Until an unlikely champion is born . . .

Pure magic!

Kylie captures the essence of her story beautifully. We have a hook *and* we have a sense of the world she's created, all in three skillfully crafted, succinct, scintillating sentences.

Yes, there is so much about the demon realm that we don't yet know. What and where is it? How is it governed? How and why did it come about? How does it link in with the world we know today? All great questions, but their answers don't form part of your synopsis. Any attempt to explain these intricacies will only tie you in knots and weigh your synopsis down with a web of information that will simply confuse the reader.

We don't need to know the functionalities of this realm to know this is going to be a riveting read. Leave the explanations for your book.

Here are some comments on how Kylie went on to write the rest of her synopsis:

> *'In all my other synopses (other than the Light Blade series), I discovered the world-building was built into my character development. I focused on the characters and wove the world-building into their descriptions or the plot rather than creating a separate world-building paragraph. And I did this mainly because the query letter or synopsis had a word limit so you couldn't dedicate separate paragraphs to this sort of thing.'*

Great tips. Showing your characters and how they behave in the world you've created is a clever and concise way of building your world into your synopsis.

Show subgenre through language and tone

What do I mean by 'subgenre'? These are the many subordinate or secondary genres within the genre of romance. Examples of these are medical, mystery, historical, suspense, time-travel, paranormal, and the list goes on.

Subgenre, and as a consequence world-building, shouldn't impact on the structure or crafting of your synopsis. What it will impact on is your choice of language and tone. Words you use in an historical or regency novel would be ill-fitting in a futuristic or sci-fi novel. The same goes for a story set in a fictional world as opposed to something set in a country foreign to your own. If your story is set in the past, don't refer to technology or scientific discoveries post that era.

By using the above rules of thumb – point of difference, KISS and brevity – no matter the setting, era or agency of your story, your synopsis should be clean, simple and easily accessible to any reader, despite their lack of knowledge of your world or characters.

World-building examples

Let's look at a series of examples across different subgenres to collect ideas on how world-building can be tackled. Any one of these methods can be adopted in your synopsis; it's a matter of choosing what works best for you and your story.

Fantasy / paranormal

Unpublished manuscript (Clare Lucy)

The battle between vampire and werewolf has raged for hundreds of years, nowhere more violently than on the streets of London. A fragile peace now holds, policed by the Guardians, a Government agency full of misfits and weirdos that no one in power admits to knowing.

Such a wealth of information in two sentences. Clare has provided a clear sense of world, of time and of place. And a sense of the war that's been raging for centuries. This is a powerful opener for any synopsis.

Post-apocalyptic romance yet to be published (Kylie Griffin)

Three hundred years have passed since The Cleansing rendered half the world's population sterile, splitting humankind – those in the Walled Cities who've retained legacies from the past and those outside reduced to hand-to-mouth existence.

Those outside the walls see a slice of heaven denied them by rank. And there are those within who view the walls as a prison, yet few are brave enough to venture outside into hell . . .

A little longer than one or two sentences, but we have a lot of critical set-up information here. We get a sense of time (three hundred years since an apocalyptic plague), a sense of disaster (in form of 'The Cleansing') and a sense of impact and ongoing conflict (humankind split in two – the haves and have-nots). Already a story is unfolding before we read on. Just brilliant!

Notice there's no in-depth discussion about 'The Cleansing' – we don't need it here. That's backstory and doesn't belong in your synopsis unless it exerts a *direct impact* on your major turning points (see Chapter 3: What's in and what's out? for more on how to identify these).

Give the reader just enough information to put context into your story and no more.

Sci-fi / other worlds

Dark Shadows (Kylie Griffin)

Let's take a look at a before-and-after example of Kylie's hook and world-building paragraph.

Before:
In unsettled times, the Vorish Confederation seek to exploit any race weaker than them. Fearing execution after the Vorish invasion of her home planet of Delrath, KATERYN INDIE, an empathic telepath, abandons her family and flees to the dubious safety of the Outer-Worlds. (43 words)

Note that Kylie has provided the reader will all the information they need about the world she's crafted for the purpose of this story. We know there is a power (the Vorish Confederation) that terrorizes the galaxy and has invaded our heroine's home planet (Delrath).

This is a great start. Now let's see if we can reorganize this information into a hook-transition-story scenario.

After:
Invasion by the Vorish Confederation means certain death to those with powers.

So, when telepath KATERYN INDIE'S home planet of Delrath is invaded, she abandons her family, trading execution for the dubious safety of the Outer-Worlds. (36 words)

Or, if you prefer:

Invasion by the Vorish Confederation means certain death to those with powers.

So, when the planet Delrath is invaded, telepath KATERYN INDIE must abandon her family, trading execution for the nebulous safety of the Outer-Worlds. (35 words)

Can you see the difference? In both rewrites, all vital information is retained, but they pack more punch than the first example. They are pacier, pithier. Hookier. And in a situation where every word counts, we've shaved eight words off our total, reducing an opening of forty-three words to thirty-five. It's a definite win-win!

Historical

As mentioned before, the language you use and the situations your characters find themselves in can provide an evocative and strong indication of genre.

A Scoundrel by Moonlight (Anna Campbell)

Justice. That's all NELL TRIM wants. For her sister and for the countless other young women the Marquess of Leath has ruined with his wildly seductive ways.

Let's take a closer look at the clever way Anna has used language to convey time period.

'*the countless young women the Marquess of Leath has ruined with his wildly seductive ways*'.

Wow. Anna has immediately drawn the reader into nineteenth century England. How? With the mention of a Marquess, we know she's describing a British nobleman ranked below a duke and above an earl. And of course we know this is pre-twentieth century, with the reference to young women's lives being *'ruined with his wildly seductive ways.'*

Is your story set in another period? If so, what terminology or words can you use in your synopsis to drop the reader straight into that era?

Regency

For those who are unsure, Regency romance is a subgenre of historical romance novels that is set during the period of the English Regency or early nineteenth century.

Untamed (Anna Cowan)

Outspoken and opinionated, KATHERINE SUTHERLAND is ill at ease amongst the fine ladies of Regency London. She is more familiar with farmers and her blunt opinions and rough manners offend polite society. Yet when she hears the scandalous rumors involving her sister and the seductive Duke of Darlington, the fiercely loyal Katherine vows to save her sister's marriage – whatever the cost.

Let's break this paragraph down and see what the language tells us. Anna uses terms such as 'fine ladies', 'Regency London' and 'polite society'. Immediately we know this is a story about classes set in regency London. Then we are introduced to the idea of 'scandalous rumors' and a 'seductive Duke'. Where else but historically would we find these two descriptors?

Every word in your synopsis has an impact. Choose those words and your wording carefully. In Anna's case, the more subtle usage of 'ill at ease' and 'blunt opinions and rough manners' help place us in an historical period. Even something as simple as whether to contract your verbs or not will make a difference to the tone, and hence hint at a time period, or even the age or class of your central characters.

Futuristic

Terminator

In a time where machines rule the world, the only hope for human survival lives in the past.

Just one sentence and straight away we know this story is set in the future and that time travel will be involved to save mankind from the machines who want to destroy it.

Powerful stuff!

The Hunger Games (Suzanne Collins)

Let's start with the logline used in promoting the movie:

May the odds be ever in your favor.

And here are a few I've created:

1. Only one can survive.

2. A game where both love and life cannot be won.

3. A game of choices: love or life?

4. In order to win, love must be lost.

Can you think of any others?

Fictional world / fantasy

Disney's *Aladdin*

In the Arabian town of Agrabah, only a prince can marry a princess.

This is a great hook and world-builder, all in one.

Arabia may not be a fictional place, but Agrabah is, and this one sentence identifies the key point of difference in this city as well as the overarching theme of Aladdin's story – only a prince can marry a princess.

This law is central to the plot. Remove it, and you remove Aladdin's motivation and his conflict. You also remove the reason he feels he can't free the genie and has to maintain his ruse of being Prince Ali. In turn, these events lead to the black moment where Jafar steals the lamp, exposes Aladdin and takes control of Agrabah.

Without this law, there is no story of *Aladdin*.

The Lion, the Witch and the Wardrobe (C.S. Lewis)

Narnia . . . a land frozen in eternal winter . . . a country waiting to be set free.

or

Four adventurers step through a wardrobe door and into winter-bound Narnia, a land enslaved by the White Witch's magic. But when all hope seems lost, the return of the Great Lion, Aslan, signals a great change . . . and a great sacrifice.

The world of Narnia is vastly different from the world we know. It's mythical, magical, a land where animals talk, dwarfs and giants roam, and humans enter from our world through inanimate objects such as a wardrobe or oil painting. It's a fascinating place, full of wonderful idiosyncrasies.

But do we need to know that Narnia is flat not round? Or that the sky is a dome that earthly creatures cannot penetrate? Or that the Narnian sun is a flaming disc that revolves around the world once daily and is thought to be inhabited by great white birds? All great detail for building the world and its uniqueness, but is it relevant for the synopsis? No.

We do, however, need to know that the world is under a spell that makes it forever winter and never Christmas. And we do need knowledge of the prophesy foretelling the end of the witch's wintry reign with the coming of Aslan and the sons of Adam and daughters of Eve. These points are intrinsic to the plot and each central character's GMC.

There is a wood between the worlds that links the many worlds of Narnia, and the white witch will become ill if she is taken there. If this fact is instrumental in the White Witch's downfall, then we need to know it. If not, then this piece of information doesn't warrant a mention in the synopsis.

Pick carefully the information you include in your synopsis. Analyze each point to ensure it has earned its place and that without it, your major turning points would make no sense.

If this is not the case, then leave it out.

Time Travel

Kate and Leopold

When a time-traveling physicist makes 1826 meet modern-day New York, a Duke and future elevator inventor meets his match in a market researcher; perfect but for one glitch – they belong to different centuries.

A wealth of information has been cleverly woven into thirty-three words. Let's pull this world-building sentence apart and see what we've discovered.

Most importantly, we know we are about to enter a story involving time travel with the reference to a 'time-traveling physicist'. Tying in with this theme, there is mention of two love interests belonging to different centuries, plus we're told that the early 1800s will meet modern times. In addition, we know in which US city the story is set – New York. We've been handed a major turning point – 'a time-travelling physicist makes 1826 meet modern-day'. And we've been given a short introduction to our central characters – an inventing Duke and a modern-day market researcher.

Who knew you could convey so much with so few words? What a great orienting paragraph. It would make a fabulous elevator pitch and identifies the high concept of the story in a clever and concise way – love across the centuries.

As an alternative, you can begin your orienting paragraph with a shorter world-building statement before creating a more in-depth outline of character GMC. Examples of shorter statements are:

1. What if your perfect match belonged to another century?

2. If Kate and Leopold lived in the same century their love would be perfect.

3. Sometimes you must cross the boundaries of time to find love.

Can you think of any others?

International

His 24-hour Wife (Rachel Bailey)

What happened in Vegas didn't stay there for CEO ADAM HAWKE and go-getter CALLIE MITCHELL.

The author of this sentence is a wizard of the short, sharp and snappy. This is a hook and a world-building statement, a misquote and a character introduction. We know something happened between Adam and Callie in Vegas, and we know they'd rather it didn't follow them when they left, but it did. Intriguing, orienting and well-crafted. A perfect lead-in to Adam and Callie's GMC.

Contemporary

How the Sheriff Was Won (Anne Gracie)

The French call it the coup de foudre *– love at first sight. But not everyone recognizes love when it hits them . . .*

Anne's opening sentence doesn't world-build or show subgenre, but boy does it hook. Immediately we get the central theme of her story. I don't know about you, but I want to know who the love interests are and why they didn't recognize love when it hit.

No matter that Anne's first sentence doesn't world-build; it has hooked its audience, and hooked them well. As long as the following sentences – where she introduces her characters and their GMC – weave in world-building cues, this works as an effective synopsis opening.

And there you have it. A look at world-building and how to incorporate it simply and seamlessly into your synopsis.

Before we move on, I'd like you to leave this chapter with two points clear in your mind. When crafting your synopsis:

1. Ensure you give a sense of the world by weaving your world-building into the plot.
2. Only show the point of differences – whether that be in your characters, your world or the rules of your world – that exert a direct impact on your plot, your major turning points and your characters.

Tempt us with a taste of your story's world without dishing up the entire repast.

Your turn . . .

See if you can create a world-building statement for these well-known stories and movies:

- » Star Wars
- » Charlotte's Web
- » The Princess Bride
- » Footloose
- » My Girl
- » Jane Eyre
- » Pride and Prejudice
- » The Time Traveler's Wife

Can you think of any others?

Take a look at your current work in progress. Are there any world-building components that you can build into a hook or orienting statement for your synopsis?

3. CENTRAL THEME

When we talk about the central theme of a novel, we are talking about the essence or premise.

The premise

This is the basis of your story. It's what happens to your characters as a result of your plot.

A great one-sentence definition of the premise is 'high concept, taking a series of complex plotlines and consolidating them into one simple idea that immediately attracts interest, and that can be quickly and easily communicated.'

In screenwriting, the premise is conveyed in both a tagline and logline. These resources are not only invaluable in helping pinpoint the crux of your novel, but they can form an important part of your synopsis.

Taglines make powerful hooks. Loglines make fabulous elevator pitches from which you should be able to extract a story's central theme and then craft your tagline. Both are invaluable on the hop, if you *just so happen* to bump into an editor or agent.

With that in mind, let's take a brief look at both.

Tagline

This is a one-sentence summary that will define the central theme of your story. A tagline should be no more than ten words.

Examples

1. Lethal in Love – Friends and enemies, can you tell the difference?

2. Murder Most Unusual – When fact melds with fiction a sadistic killer is born.

3. The Princess Bride – When true love is the only thing that will save you.

4. When Harry met Sally – Men and women can never be friends.

5. Beauty and the Beast – When love is brave and beautiful, and more than skin deep.

Logline

Usually three or four sentences long, a logline summarizes the plot and the central characters' GMCs, and it give a sense of higher stakes, i.e., what the characters stand to gain or lose *personally* if things don't go their way.

To construct or not to construct?

Why construct a tagline and logline before writing your story or synopsis?

This may seem like a tangent from the topic of writing the perfect synopsis, but if you don't have a good grasp of your central theme, the building blocks of your synopsis could very easily come tumbling down.

So, what are the benefits of adding this one step into your synopsis writing process?

Because loglines and taglines:

» identify the crux of your novel, i.e., the central theme, the central characters and their respective GMCs

» provide focus as you write, i.e., pin-point the central theme and the central characters' GMCs, ensuring your story and characters remain true to the plot and their path

» form an elevator pitch that will sell your story to an editor or publisher.

Key elements of a logline

1. Characters
   » Who are the central characters and what are their goals?
   » Use descriptive adjectives instead of your characters' names.

2. Conflict
   » Who or what is the main obstacle preventing the main character from achieving their goal?
3. Difference
   » What makes your story stand out?
4. Setting
   » Hint at the setting, time period and genre if they are not immediately obvious.
5. Action
   » This is your plot, i.e., something needs to be happening to somebody.

Note: To evoke emotion and create images that will remain in your reader's mind, make sure you use active, emotive and descriptive words. To see some examples, take a look at Chapter 10: Refining your synopsis, Evocative language.

Examples
Lethal in Love (Michelle Somers)

When a serial killer leads the Melbourne police force astray, an instinct-driven detective teams up with a sexy, scoop-hungry reporter to catch the murderer before she becomes his next victim.

Let's break this logline down and see that it contains all five key elements.

Characters: an instinct-driven detective and a scoop-hungry reporter.

Conflict: a serial killer is leading the Melbourne police force astray and threatens the detective's life unless she can catch him first.

Distinction: *Lethal in Love* is more than just a romance. It's full of suspense and mystery and the female protagonist wields the gun.

Setting: Melbourne, Australia.

Action: Detective and reporter must work together to catch a killer before the detective becomes the next victim.

Murder Most Unusual (Michelle Somers)

When a Melbourne serial killer breathes literature's gruesome murders to life, can a quirky romance novelist and conflicted homicide detective fight the attraction between them, all-the-while fighting the killer determined to destroy them both?

This information-packed sentence ticks all the boxes.

What if we tease the ideas out and give a little more information, replacing the single sentence with three? I've included my characters' names here, which makes this a cross between a logline and a story back cover blurb, but it will give you an idea of how much scope you have when crafting.

Romantic suspense novelist STACEY HOLLAND lives in a fictitious world where the mortality of her characters is governed by a tap on her keyboard. Homicide detective CHASE DURANT's cases are real and gritty and one wrong move could be his last. When their two worlds collide, and fiction melds with fact, can they fight the attraction raging between them, all-the-while fighting the killer determined to destroy them both?

Jane Eyre (Charlotte Brontë)

In an English manor, a 'plain-Jane' governess thaws the heart of her austere employer and finds love, only to discover he's hiding a terrible secret.

Gone with the Wind (Margaret Mitchell)

A manipulative Southern belle pines for the wrong man, refusing to give in to her attraction for a dashing blockade runner during the American Civil War.

Beauty and the Beast (Disney)

A young woman offers herself as captive in her father's place, unaware her terrifying captor is a prince trapped by magic in a beast's body.

Can you think of any others?

Once you've created both logline and tagline, continue crafting your synopsis. Refer to them as you write to ensure your central character arcs and your story's central theme are clearly represented in both the orienting paragraphs as well as the body of your synopsis.

The central theme can make a great hook – hence providing another use for your tagline – but there may be times when world-building or character GMC packs more punch. In these cases, make sure your opening paragraphs allude to or contain reference to the high concept of your story. Then in your concluding paragraphs, refer back to this concept and clearly demonstrate your plot resolution and conclusion, as well as your story and character arc.

A great example of this 'full-circle' effect is the movie, *When Harry Met Sally*. The tagline or central theme is the lynchpin of the plot. Every major turning point in the story relates back to this central theme. And in those last climactic scenes, when Harry and Sally finally get their happy ever after, the central theme is proven, categorically – men and women can never just be friends.

Your turn . . .

Why not pick a classic novel or movie and see if you can craft both tagline and logline. Or revisit the world-building statements you made earlier and see if you can create a tagline and logline that fits with those stories.

Then look at your current work in progress and see if you can do the same.

MOVIE/BOOK TITLE:

CENTRAL THEME:

TAGLINE:

LOGLINE:

---

4. CENTRAL CHARACTERS

The fourth and final component of your orientation paragraphs is the introduction of the main characters in your story. On the surface this introduction seems a simple task:

> *Reader, this is Lucy. Lucy, this is your reader* <wipes hands, job done, smiles relief>.

Okay, I may have injected a hint of tongue-in-cheek here, but this example demonstrates one vital point – introducing your characters is NOT simple. It's not something that can be whipped up in a few seconds so you can move onto the juicy stuff – like the plot.

Your characters will either make or break your story. Get them right and you'll be that much closer to a winner novel. Get them wrong, and let's just say it's akin to offering your readers a cardboard cut-out – flat, boring and dismally unimaginative.

Introducing your characters in a synopsis is not a matter of telling us who they are and what they do for a living. We need to know more. And, as always, the information you impart in these vital first paragraphs will demonstrate how rich your story really is. And will be one of the deciding factors for whether the reader, i.e., the editor or agent, reads on, and whether they recognize something special in your characters that makes your story marketable and interesting for a wider readership.

What to include in a synopsis

What should you include about your central characters in a synopsis? Note, once again, that term 'central characters'. This equates to your protagonists – the characters whose journeys are featured in your story. In romance, this encompasses your central love interests. In a classic romance, it's your hero and heroine. What it doesn't include is the loyal best friend, the whiney sister, the over-bearing mother, the over-protective father, the bossy brother . . . do I need to go on?

Yes, your wonderful couple may be surrounded by a world of colorful and challenging support characters, but for the purpose of the synopsis, the editor/agent is solely interested in your hero and heroine's story. Secondary characters only get a mention so far as they *impact on the development of the plot or the romance*, and even then, any mention should be fleeting. This rule also applies to stories that fall outside the romance genre. If a character propels the story or protagonist's character arc forward, then they earn a mention in your synopsis.

What do the editor or agent need to know about your starring couple? The bare minimum, as it relates to the plot and their developing relationship.

The bare bones of this can be summarized as Goal, Motivation, Conflict – or more lovingly referred to by those in the industry as a character's 'GMC'.

I have already made several references to GMC, but let's take a closer look at what it really means.

What is GMC?

GMC refers to Goal, Motivation, Conflict and is the lynchpin of your characters and your story. Whether you're a plotter, pantser, plantser or scener, it's imperative you have an in-depth understanding of your characters' GMCs before your story is complete. Each character in your story MUST have a goal, motivation and conflict. Without them, they are nothing more than the cardboard cut-out I mentioned earlier.

GMC is the tinder fueling the fire, the reason you have a story and your characters have a journey before they win their happy ever after. GMC is the layers in your characters – it gives them depth, dimension and direction.

GMC will either win you or lose you that coveted publishing contract.

So, let's break it down and take a closer look.

Goal

What does your character want?

This goal needs to be important enough to drive your character through the story. It must be measurable, urgent and give your character a reason to act.

Example: *Lucy wants to build a children's cancer wing.*

Motivation

Why does your character want this goal?

There must be a reason strong enough to make them need this goal above all else. It's the driving force behind your character's actions. It's the 'if I don't get this *thing*, my life is over' scenario.

Dig deep into your character's mind, deep into their past to find this reason. It should be personal, it should be relatable and it should be real. Motivation is a big part of what makes the reader empathize with your character and it drives them to read on until your character has won whatever it is that they desire.

This desire can't be a flimsy, 'I'd like this, but if I don't get it, oh well, never mind'. That won't invest your readers in your story. Make the motivation strong, significant and substantial. Make it matter.

Example: *Lucy wants to build a children's cancer wing to honor her daughter's memory.*

Conflict

What is preventing your character from getting this goal?

This is the seemingly impossible obstacle or obstacles that keep the character from attaining the goal until they've proven themselves worthy through struggle and hard choices. The lynchpin of lynchpins.

Make your character work and learn and grow to achieve their goal. The more you make them forge through hell to get there, the more the reader will champion for them to win. If the goal is obtainable and well within reach, there is no story. If nothing is preventing Lucy from gaining the building contract she so desperately desires, then she has no journey, the story has no substance and there's really no reason for the reader to read on.

Conflict places the reader on tenterhooks, makes them worry, panic even. The conflict must make it seem impossible that the character will ever reach their goal, impossible that they'll find their happy ever after, impossible that the detective will catch the killer and solve the case. The conflict is what makes the reader turn page after page late into the night. It robs their concentration and ingrains the character's dilemma in their minds long after they've closed the book and tried to move onto more pressing tasks. It's what brings the reader back to your story, hungry to discover what your character will do next.

> **Example:** *Lucy wants to build a children's cancer wing to honor her daughter's memory but she must first raise the funds and engage the architect who threatens to make her lose her head and break her heart.*

More often than not, a heroine's conflict will be in contrast to the hero's. An example of this could be:

> The heroine shuns commitment and love because the only relationships she's witnessed are disasters. But her sister has just died and to win custody of her niece she must provide a stable home environment. That environment includes a husband and prospective father-figure for her niece.

> The hero craves commitment and love to fill the gap his family left when they died in a house fire. He was adopted at age five and he's just lost the last living parent he remembers. He meets the girl who was his best friend before his life turned bad and he had to move. She symbolizes that stability and love he craves, and he's determined to marry her, but for the fact that she's anti-love and wants a marriage in name only.

Talk about conflict!

Or, maybe your central characters' GMCs are similar, and as a result, their conflicts are mirrored or linked in some way. An example of this could be:

> Both hero and heroine want the same promotion. The heroine needs it so she can afford a better care facility for her elderly, disabled mother and the hero needs it for validation, to prove he's not the failure his father always said he was. Their conflict? Only one of them can win that coveted position.

Riveting reading if teamed with the right plot.

Now that all this is, hopefully, starting to make sense, let's throw a spanner in the works.

External vs. Internal GMC

It is important to realize that there are two kinds of GMC – external and internal – and each character will have both. Let's explore the differences.

External GMC

This is something tangible that your character wants to achieve in your story. If your character's goal is tactile – if they can see it, smell it, taste it, feel it or hear it – then it's external. Examples include a promotion, a baby, a relationship, escaping a particular situation, catching a killer or simply catching a partner.

Make sure that whatever your character's external goal, their driving force or motivation is a strong one.

Internal GMC

This relates to your character's state of mind and any doubts they may have in regards to achieving their external goal. If your character's goal is emotionally driven, then it's internal. Examples include proving something to themselves or someone else, winning love, notice or acknowledgement, overcoming doubts or low self-image. I'm sure you can think of more once you sit down and start listing.

The internal GMC forms a huge part of your character arc. By the end of your story, your character will have achieved their goal and overcome whatever internal conflict previously held them back.

Example

Imagine your character's external goal is to find the Excalibur Sword and return it to its rightful owner, bringing peace and harmony to the kingdom. What if they've never stepped foot outside the kingdom? What if their every action has been dictated from birth, what if they've never had to act or think for themselves before? Their lack of self-confidence and belief in their ability will be something they must overcome before they realise their goal and complete their quest.

See how external and internal GMCs are interlinked?

GMC example

Let's formulate a GMC statement and use it to create our synopsis orienting paragraphs.

A basic GMC statement will follow this structure:

[Character] **WANTS** [goal] **BECAUSE** [motivation] **BUT** [conflict].

Applying this principle to our earlier example of Lucy, this sentence would read:

> Lucy WANTS to build a children's cancer wing BECAUSE she wants to honor her daughter's memory BUT she must first raise the funds and engage the architect who threatens to make her lose her head and break her heart.

Now let's further explore GMCs for both Lucy and her counterpart, Jack.

I've found the most visual and most effective way of doing this is a table format. Identifying both internal and external goals, motivations and conflicts for each of these central characters will generate the building blocks necessary to construct the GMC portion of our orienting paragraphs.

Lucy's Love Lessons (Michelle Somers)

Name: LUCY CONNOR
Adjectives: Jaded, distrustful
Occupation: Carpenter / Acting-CEO of her father's construction company

	EXTERNAL	INTERNAL
GOAL	**WANTS** to build a children's cancer wing at the city hospital. **WANTS** to retain her position as CEO of her step-father's construction company past the 3 month stipulation in his will.	**WANTS** to guard her heart from hurt. **WANTS** to prove her worth. She has three months to show that she's as able and qualified to run her father's company as any man.
MOTIVATION	**BECAUSE** she wants to honor the memory of the child she lost to cancer. **BECAUSE** the job gives her purpose – a reason to wake up every morning. **BECAUSE** jobs don't die and leave you, or lie and undermine every ounce of your trust.	**BECAUSE** her heart broke when her husband lied about his gambling and he lost the savings needed for her daughter's cancer treatment. **BECAUSE** when her father cheated and then left her mother, he left her too. **BECAUSE** the job fills the void of family and loss in her life. And the job doesn't lie, people do . . .
CONFLICT	**BUT** she must raise the funds and engage the architect that both hospital and council have stipulated – an architect who wants more than her broken heart can give. **BUT** after 3 months, the all-male board can vote her out unless she proves herself worthy, and to do this she must work with a man who undermines her need to remain emotionally detached.	**BUT** the board and every man she encounters doubts her ability, just as her ex-husband did. And even her step-father – he only conceded to the 3 month probation at the insistence of her mother. **BUT** she's never undertaken such a large project before, and she must overcome secret fears of failure and her suspicion that perhaps the doubters are right after all . . .

Name: JACK SMITH
Adjectives: Lonely, determined
Occupation: Architect

	EXTERNAL	INTERNAL
G O A L	**WANTS** to build a life outside the work that has consumed him for the past ten years. **WANTS** to find the right woman to create a family and a life with.	**WANTS** to banish the loneliness and bring purpose back into his life. **WANTS** to feel a sense of permanency and belonging, a sense of home, to make him feel alive.
M O T I V A T I O N	**BECAUSE** he's been alone since his family was killed in a house fire over twenty-five years ago. **BECAUSE** his recent cancer scare made him realize life should be about more than just work.	**BECAUSE** architecture and his work life no longer fills the hole losing his family left. **BECAUSE** after staring down the barrel of a possible terminal cancer diagnosis, he wants his legacy to be more than just work. **BECAUSE** he wants a wife and kids who will love him when he's there and miss him when he's gone.
C O N F L I C T	**BUT** the woman he wants doesn't want him back – all she's after are building plans and a contract. **BUT** if he shares details of his brush with cancer, will she be willing to take a chance on him? Given she lost her daughter to the disease. Given she's scared of loving and losing again.	**BUT** he can't open up and let people in. He's used to holding people at arm's length to protect himself, to prevent feeling loss again like he did when his family died. Now he's found the woman he wants, he's not even sure where to start. Or whether she'd want him given the risk the cancer could return.

Note how closely internal and external GMC are linked. Not only are physical barriers holding Lucy and Jack back from achieving their goals, but there are internal/emotional barriers as well: doubts, insecurities, old hurts exerting their influence on the present. These form a key part of a character's GMC and as a result they form a critical part of the orienting paragraphs of your synopsis.

If your character's GMC is clear in your manuscript, and your mind, this table should be a straightforward translation of information.

If you're struggling to identify internal and/or external GMC, it may pay to revisit your manuscript. Do you have a clear understanding of your characters, their goals, their motivations, their conflicts? Are they developed enough in your story? If not, deepen them. Strengthen them. Give them more purpose, more drive. Then give the table another go.

Once your characters' GMCs are clearly defined, formulate your orienting paragraphs bearing in mind the rules of KISS, brevity and language choice.

Let's look at some before-and-after examples of an old synopsis I have on file and how I applied these principles.

Worth the Risk (Michelle Somers)

First draft:
ALISE RIERDAN divorced her controlling husband three years ago and suffered depression so debilitating she withdrew from life and the world. That and being betrayed by the boy she loved in high school, when he sold drugs to the driver of a car who killed her sister, have made her distrustful of men and relationships. She may not be interested in commitment, but she is interested in making up for the fun and flirting she missed in the past. All she needs is a dose of the ever elusive orgasm, and a sexy man to deliver it. (97 words)

Second draft:
ALISE RIERDAN doesn't want commitment or a relationship. Nothing past the fun and flirting she missed in the past. Betrayed by the boy she loved in high school when he sold drugs to her sister's killer, then tied to a controlling husband until she divorced him three years ago, walking away in a cloud of depression and self-loathing, she doesn't trust men. That doesn't mean she can't enjoy them, fleetingly, and take pleasure in an orgasm or several, before walking away, heart intact and head in control. (87 words)

Final draft:

It's three years since ALISE RIERDAN's divorce from a control-freak and the resulting depression. Ten since her best friend and prom date sold drugs to the man who killed her sister. Relationships with men she doesn't want, need or trust, unless they're the fleeting kind. So, it's time for fun and experiences missed in her youth – the ever elusive orgasm and a sexy man to deliver it. (67 words)

The last example is leaner and pacier, yet we have all the information necessary to know exactly where Alise is at when her story starts. She's emerged from a black time in her life and is ready to make up for lost opportunities. She doesn't trust men, but she's willing to have a sex-no-strings fling. And she's sewn her heart up so tight, it will take a special man with a bucketload of patience to pry it open again.

This paragraph works as is, but if we wanted to add an opening hook, here's a couple of possibilities:

1. ALISE RIERDAN wants an orgasm without entanglements.

2. Sex without strings won't break a girl's heart.

Can you think of any others? What hooks or high concept ideas can you come up with to enhance this synopsis?

Your turn . . .

Now that you have the foundation for Lucy and Jack's GMC, see if you can formulate your own orientation paragraphs. As you write, remember the rules of thumb: KISS and brevity, and select language and tone to represent subgenre. This story could be either contemporary romance or romcom. See if you can write one version of each, using the same GMC but different vocabulary and voice. Try to hook your reader and inject interest-value into every sentence, while capturing the essence that is the story, as well as both Lucy and Jack's goal, motivation and conflict.

Now build your own GMC table. Choose a central character from your current work in progress or a favorite movie or novel. Ensure you link internal and external GMC. Demonstrate how the character's internal conflicts are holding them back from achieving their external goal.

Name:

Adjectives:

Occupation:

	EXTERNAL	**INTERNAL**
G O A L	WANTS	WANTS
M O T I V A T I O N	BECAUSE	BECAUSE
C O N F L I C T	BUT	BUT

Now look at my examples of orienting paragraphs for Lucy and Jack and see how they compare to yours.

Good and not-so-good examples of orientation paragraphs

Keeping in mind what we have just learned about hooks, world-building, central theme and central characters, and applying the GMC information from the previous table, let's take a critical look at the following orientation paragraph:

a. Example of a bad orientation paragraph

LUCY CONNOR became CEO of her step-father's construction company when he died and she has three months to prove her worth before she can be voted out. The all-male board was about as happy as her ex-husband, who disapproved of her more senior position and who lied about his gambling debts until all their savings were gone – the savings they needed to pay for their daughter's life-saving cancer treatment. Now Lucy wants to prove she can do the job as well as any man. First up is a new cancer wing for the children's hospital in memory of her dead daughter. But she needs a few things organized before that can happen. She needs to find enough money for the project, sign up the architect approved by both hospital and council, and get her plans approved through the planning process, all the while dodging advances from the man who could unravel every emotional safeguard she has employed to keep her heart intact. (161 words)

A few comments about this example:

It's long, clumsy and contains way too much extraneous information.

Where is the GMC? It's in there – somewhere – but it's difficult to decipher among all the ramble.

Where do the principle problems lie?

Content: We don't need to know about Lucy's step-father's construction company in the first sentence. And depending on how vital it is to her GMC, we might not need to know it was her step-father's company at all. However, it is important to know she's a CEO, as it tells us something about her character – her business acumen, as well as her personal strength, confidence and ability in relation to her work. The fact that she has three months to prove herself before she can be voted out injects a race-against-time impetus that highlights the urgency and tension of her situation.

In terms of Lucy's ex-husband, all we need to know is that he's *disapproving, lying and history*. Anything about him that doesn't relate back to her GMC doesn't belong in the synopsis.

Pacing: Your synopsis should be pacey in the same way your story should be. That means paring it back to the basics. Read it aloud. Cut out extraneous words. If you can say something with one word instead of two or three, do it.

Instead of '*she needs to find enough money for the project*' you could write '*she must raise the funds*'.

'*But she needs a few things organized before that can happen*' can be deleted.

Let's say you were keeping the above sentence in. You could replace '*before that can happen*' with the word '*first*'. You've just cut three words from your synopsis without losing meaning.

Now let's take a look how to craft it better.

b. Examples of well-written orientation paragraphs

Example 1: the simple version
Jaded and divorced acting-CEO LUCY CONNOR wants to build a children's cancer wing in memory of her daughter. But first she must raise the funds, engage an architect and gain planning approval, all the while proving herself worthy of the position past her three-month trial period.

The job is no longer enough for architect and cancer survivor JACK SMITH. He wants a wife and children – a family – to fill the void left after his parents and brother died in a house fire when he was a child. But the woman he's fallen for hasn't fallen in return and he needs to convince her to trust him before the completion of their contract means she's free to walk away and never look back. (122 words)

Example 2: a little more complex

Acting-CEO LUCY CONNOR needs a man like she needs the disdain of her construction company's board. Men lie, cheat, make you doubt yourself and then they gamble your savings so you can't afford your daughter's cancer treatments. Now she's rid of her double-dealing husband, she doesn't need another man to take his place. All she needs is the board's vote to remain CEO, as well as funds, plans and approval for a new children's cancer wing to ensure her daughter's memory will never die.

Architect and cancer survivor JACK SMITH needs a wife and kids to fill the void left by his health scare and the house fire that ripped his parents and brother from his life. Only problem is, the first woman to spark his interest is less than interested. She won't discuss anything but work, and wants nothing more from him than a set of building plans and a contract.

So he drafts a little contract of his own . . . (161 words)

Example 3: a little more creative

Lies never stay secret forever.

A lesson acting-CEO LUCY CONNOR's ex-husband taught her for two long years until she walked out, leaving him and any idea of love behind. Life with just work may not be full, but it is safe – she'll never travel the marriage and kids route again. All she needs is the board's vote to remain CEO and their endorsement for a new cancer wing honoring the memory of her beloved daughter. If only she can raise the funds, employ an architect and get planning approval while safeguarding her heart from the man who threatens to steal it.

Architect and cancer survivor JACK SMITH is looking for love, marriage and a family like the one he lost as a child. Death's taunts have left him a new mantra – live life to the fullest because you never know when it'll be gone. He's set his sights on the sexy CEO, but she wants nothing from him past building plans and a contract. Determined to show her the error of her ways, he devises a new contract – dates in exchange for designing her hospital wing. If only he didn't have to keep his ultimate goal – marriage and kids – a secret. (201 words)

Example 4: a lot more complex

Lies never stay secret forever.

A lesson acting-CEO LUCY CONNOR's ex-husband taught her for two long years until she walked out, leaving him and any idea of love behind. She needs a man like she needs the disdain of her construction company's board. Men lie and cheat. They make you doubt yourself, and they gamble your savings until you can't afford your daughter's cancer treatments. Now she's rid of her ex, she doesn't need another man to take his place. All she needs is the board's vote to cement her CEO status and the funds, plans and approval for a new children's cancer wing to ensure her daughter's memory will never die.

Architect and cancer survivor JACK SMITH is sick of the solo life. Orphaned at five, he craves the family he had so briefly. Life won't wait for happiness to call – it's his job to find it. Then he meets Lucy and something about the sassy, sarcastic CEO makes him want to delve beneath her prickles to find the warmth he's sure lurks beneath. If only she'd let conversation span beyond building plans and contracts. If only the one secret he holds wasn't the one thing that could tear them apart. (202 words)

Of course, the version you use will depend on the final length of your synopsis; and synopsis length will be determined by the submission guidelines, or in the case of competitions, the entry guidelines.

A three-page synopsis will give more leeway than a one-page synopsis.

Regardless of its length, make sure you inject your voice into your synopsis. Ensure your opening paragraphs hook, orient and clarify your central theme and your central characters' GMCs. Finally, always check that these paragraphs contain the four key components:

1. Hook
2. World-building
3. Central theme
4. Central characters

Now that you've structured the perfect orientation paragraphs, it's time to build the body of your synopsis.

CHAPTER 3
MAJOR TURNING POINTS

A major turning point is a significant event that impacts character growth and/or the direction of your storyline. Within a romance, there will be specific plot points that are critical in the development of the relationship between your hero and heroine as well. These are the turning points that must make it into your synopsis. Choose the major plot points, the ones that really make a difference. The points that showcase your characters' GMCs, move them forward in their journey and bring them one or more steps closer to their goals and happy ever after.

In fiction outside the romance genre, include the plot points most closely related to your story's central theme, as well as those that demonstrate character arc and your central character's progress toward achieving their goal.

Major turning points for all fiction novels

This list comprises ten turning points present in all good fiction novels, romance or otherwise.

1. **Inciting incident** – an event that sparks the central character's need to achieve their goal, propelling them into a journey that is your plot.
2. **Opportunity knocks** – like a metaphorical door opening, opportunity arises that makes movement toward a character's goal seem possible.
3. **Fork in the road** – marks the central character's choice and reaffirmation of commitment to their goal.

4. **Progress / false progress** – something happens that leads the character to take control and forge forward in their quest, making the goal seem within reach.
5. **Higher stakes (no turning back now)** – stakes toward achieving the goal are heightened and the central character is too invested to turn back now. Examples include major financial, physical or emotional commitments toward achieving their goal, races against time and threats to personal or emotional well-being if they fail.
6. **All is lost** – central character encounters an extreme setback. At this point they are furthermost from achieving their goal.
7. **The moment of truth** – a key moment in a central character's inner journey where they face their fears and make a decision. The outcome of this moment determines how this character will act in the climax.
8. **Climax** – central character gathers resources for a no-holds-barred showdown toward achieving their goal.
9. **Resolution** – a story's ending, whether it be happy or something more tragic or bittersweet.
10. **Conclusion** – a snapshot of the central character in their new world. This will be in contrast to their world at the onset of their story.

Major turning points in romance

For the purposes of this book, which is tailored toward romance synopsis creation, I've included these romance-specific turning point categories. These turning points have the potential to fall under one or several of the headings above, depending on when they occur in your story.

1. First time the central characters cross paths in the story.
2. First kiss.
3. First sparks of trust.

4. First or pivotal heart's talk – sharing something personal, especially relating to GMC.
5. First time they make love.
6. Black moment.
7. Any major, pivotal shift in their relationship.
8. Any major 'aha!' moment in relation to their goals or their relationship – link these with the plot point that triggered them. This includes the moment each central character realizes they're in love.
9. Any major stuff-ups – times they get things wrong or stumble – that set them back in terms of their goals and/or the relationship.

What to keep in mind while crafting turning points

1. Tell, don't show

Bet you never thought you'd hear this rule in relation to writing! This is one of the major differences between story and synopsis. In a synopsis, you don't have leeway, or words, to wax lyrical on your plot and characters. Remember, also, that your audience – editors and agents – are extremely busy people. They want to get to the crux of your story and how this affects your characters, fast.

So, if a plot point angers your character, say they are angry; if they feel let down, say they are disappointed – or better still, say they are enraged or disillusioned. Just because you don't show doesn't mean you can't use evocative language to set the scene and mood. Demonstrate your expertise as a writer by telling your reader how your characters feel with emotion and power.

2. Not all turning points make it into your synopsis

The trick to writing a stellar synopsis lies not so much in what to include, but in *what to leave out*. If you incorporate every change, every plot point, every twist, turn, action and reaction, all you do is retell your entire story. This is unnecessary for a piece of writing defined as '*a **summary** that breaks down your story's **central plot**, introducing the **central characters** in a **concise** but interesting way*'.

3. Only include plot points that affect the central characters

As I mentioned earlier, include plot points as they unfold in your story and only if they relate to your central characters' growth and/ or their developing relationship. Provide a simple and streamlined outline of your central plot. Sub-plots and side-issues have no place here. Anything that takes the reader away from that single track will only serve to confuse and complicate.

4. Don't include secondary characters' stories

Although we have touched upon this before, it is too important not to reiterate: secondary or support characters should not feature here, unless they exert a direct impact on your central characters and their journey. Even then, I wouldn't suggest naming these characters unless it's absolutely necessary for clarity.

What's in and what's out?

Most writers would rather visit the dentist than write a synopsis; even a root-canal looks appealing when weighed up against writing the poor, misunderstood synopsis. In part, this reaction stems from the decision of what plot points to include.

This is the bane of most writers' synopsis-writing experiences: with a story that's a web of twists and turns, which do you include in the synopsis and which can you afford to leave out? Identifying key turning points is a tricky business, and hard-and-fast rules only go so far in helping you decide. Experience helps, though to gain that experience you need a series of synopses under your belt; only then will the process become second nature.

The first step is to make a list of your turning points. I find this easier to tackle as I write, rather than waiting until the end of the book, when I have a full manuscript to wade through. But you can do either. Or you can do it as part of your plotting process before you write your book. It's really what works best for you.

So, how to start? It's as simple as this. As you build your story, note each scene that marks a critical point in your plot or a pivotal change in the development of your central characters' relationship. Once you have your list, it's then a matter of cataloguing each turning point – where does it fit in terms of the arc of both your story, your plot and your characters? And does it belong in your synopsis or can you safely exclude it without losing the essence of your plot, relationship development and character growth.

Identifying the stages of your story will not only help you write a rock-your-socks-off synopsis, it will also help ascertain whether your story has all the elements necessary to make it a rock-your-socks-off success.

Structure of turning point paragraphs

This is the place most people tend to come unstuck. You've written a set of amazing orientation paragraphs, hooked the reader and built your world. You've introduced your characters, done a mighty fine job of identifying their GMC and showing it simply and succinctly.

You've short-listed your major turning points, but now you need to insert them into the synopsis and show how they drive the story and your characters' growing relationship.

How? The best way to approach these critical parts of your synopsis is by paring each turning point down to its skeletal beginnings. Each plot-based paragraph should contain one or two plot points that relate to and/or lead up to the turning point in your story. These turning points or plot-based paragraphs are the building blocks of the body of your synopsis – each one a bone or series of bones that when connected with their partners will form the skeletal framework of your story.

But how to connect them? Tendons, of course. Or in our case, the analysis – something many forget when crafting their synopsis. Once you've written your plot points, it's important to analyze how these events drive the story, how they affect your central characters and their progress toward their individual goals, as well as their developing relationship.

Sounds easy, right? *Wrong*. Sounds messy and convoluted and just plain confusing. So let's break this step down further into its individual parts.

Here is a simple six-step method that will see you through each paragraph, ensuring you capture all the necessary information for your synopsis.

Six-step structure for major turning points

1. **Plot**
   - » What plot point led to this event taking place?
   - » What goal does this relate to?
2. **Character**
   - » Who is driving this plot point?
3. **Action**
   - » What action do they take as a result of this plot point?
4. **Motivation**
   - » What motivated the action?
5. **Reaction**
   - » How does the instigator feel during? After? What are their thoughts?
   - » How does the receiver react to this action?
   - » How do they feel? Show emotion?
6. **Impact**
   - » What impact or change does this action have on the central characters' ongoing relationship or their choice of direction in terms of attaining their goal?

These questions not only assist in the decision of which turning points deserve a place in your synopsis, but also in structuring your turning point paragraphs. For each turning point on your list, ask yourself these questions and if the answers don't directly impact on plot arc, character arc or romance arc, you should be able to safely leave out the point. If, however, a turning point is directly responsible for another turning point that does affect plot, character or romance arc, bundle these two turning points together into a paragraph and deal with them simply and succinctly.

Let's take a look at each of these major turning points for romance in greater detail.

I. THE MEET CUTE

The first major turning point in a romance is often the first meeting, or 'meet cute', a term originating from the film industry that seems to be slowly spilling into the writing world.

A 'meet cute' can be defined as '... *a fictional scene, typically in film or television, in which a future romantic couple meets for the first time in a way that is considered adorable, entertaining or amusing.*'

Those last three adjectives are important. This first meeting will either hook the interest of a potential editor or agent and invest them in your characters and the promise of their relationship, or it will lose them completely. Our aim, of course, is the first of these possibilities – both as we write our 'meet cute' into our manuscript and then as we translate it into our synopsis.

Purpose of the first meeting

This first, pivotal turning point will often form part of or be connected in some way to the inciting incident of your story.

The meet cute serves several purposes:

- » Establishes the central characters.
- » Sets the romantic conflict in motion.

» Creates a memorable moment for your characters.
» Creates a memorable moment for your readers.

And how do we ensure that this first meeting is memorable and meaningful? Make the moment genuine, but distinctive. Make it fresh, make it sparkle and make it uniquely yours. That means avoiding clichéd circumstances (such as two people colliding around a corner), forced plots (that is, contrivances that don't suit the character or circumstances) and pettiness (trifling conflicts, i.e., an argument for the sake of showing conflict).

If your story dictates one of those clichéd first meetings, give your version a little spice or a twist. Shake it up and make it different. Make something about it stand out, even if it's only the characters, their interaction and/or their reaction to each other.

Examples
Disney's *Aladdin*

The first time Princess Jasmine meets Aladdin, she's disguised and pretending to be a commoner to escape life as a royal for just a few precious hours. Aladdin is a street urchin, and in their first face-to-face moments, he saves her, whisking her out of danger and into his own world. Their connection is immediate, but we know from earlier scenes that in Agrabah only a prince can marry a princess. Their relationship is doomed before it has a chance to begin.

When Harry Met Sally

In this hilarious meet cute, Harry and Sally share a ride from University of Chicago to New York City. Their banter is engaging and conflictual, cementing the central theme – men and women can't be friends – and setting the tone for the remainder of their story and rollercoaster relationship.

The Proposal

The opening scenes of this movie show both Margaret and Andrew getting ready for work in their own, very individual lives. 'Ice queen' Margaret storms into the office and fires a fellow editor before informing Andrew he must take on his ex-colleague's work over the weekend. We sense their coworkers' regard for Andrew and their distaste toward Margaret; and we see Margaret coldly manipulate Andrew into not only lying to her superiors about a fake engagement, but to his family as well.

Such a powerful introduction to both characters, and such a conflict-packed set-up. Within seconds I'm questioning how they'll ever move past their dislike and disdain for each other to find their happy ever after.

Translating the first meeting into the synopsis

Lucy's Love Lessons (Michelle Somers)

Earlier I introduced you to Lucy Connor, a jaded acting-CEO of her step-father's building company. From the opening paragraphs of our synopsis, we know that Lucy is working hard to prove herself in a man's world and retain her position after her three month probation. In that time she intends to finalize plans for a new children's cancer wing in memory of her daughter. She is single-minded and determined, and uninterested in men until she meets architect, Jack Smith . . .

Let's look at a possible meet cute scenario for these two future love interests:

Lucy calls a meeting with the tendered architectural firm. Their sexy architect walks in and whoa! *Goodbye brain function. Jack Smith fills the room, and her vision, all too perfectly. Definitely a man to steer clear of if her career and heart are to remain intact. She'll focus on business, what needs to be done, then leave. But Jack's determined to flirt. Won't take her seriously. Like most men she meets in business. Like her ex.*

Jack oozes charisma and charm, but Lucy rebuffs every advance. He suggests dinner. She declines and terminates the meeting, angry he won't respect her position. Angry she even cares. Lucy determines to avoid the man at all costs. Next meeting she'll pass both file and frustrating architect over to her very capable, very stern PA.

Exasperated and no closer to snagging Lucy's interest, Jack leaves with a stack of notes for the building design. Lucky he doesn't give in that easy. Lucy ticks every box on his perfect wife list, presses all the right buttons, and a few more to boot. They make a winning team – her tenacity, his drive. She'll figure it out soon enough.

As a first draft, this covers all the bases. We know what events took place, who was involved and how each party feels about the interaction. And we know what action they intend to take to bring them closer to their ultimate goal.

Depending on your final word count, these paragraphs can be cut back or expanded. But regardless what you do at that final editing stage, make sure as you cut you don't cut the emotion, the drama or interest-value of the scene, and most of all, make sure you retain your unique style of writing and your voice.

Your turn . . .

If *Lucy's Love Lessons* was your story, and this was your synopsis, how would you write this first meeting? Why not give it a go now?

Why not write a 'meet cute' paragraph for your current work in progress?

Remember this is the first time your central characters will hit the page together. Make the moment *zing*. Ensure you maintain tone and voice specific to the genre, and incorporate the six-step structure for major turning points. Choose language that will evoke emotion and tension, and show any and all conflict in relation to each character's GMC.

And have fun!

MEET CUTE BREAKDOWN

PLOT:

CHARACTER:

ACTION:

MOTIVATION:

REACTION:

IMPACT:

MEET CUTE PARAGRAPH

2. THE FIRST KISS

The first kiss is usually one of the first moments of physical connection between your central characters, one of the first moments of intimacy. Above all, it's an admission of – or at the very least, a concession to – the attraction that exists between them. And it's possibly the first time they've given in to that attraction. As a result, this is one of those magic moments that categorically belongs in your synopsis.

The first kiss can form part of opportunity knocks, a fork in the road or making progress, depending on when in your story it takes place and which major plot point it is linked to.

Once your couple has kissed, things will change between them. They can't go back or forget how they felt, how they reacted, how good or bad or indifferent the experience was. These emotions, these thoughts, need to be shown in this paragraph. How do both characters *feel* before and after the kiss? What do they *think* before and after? How has this event shaped their behavior generally, as well as toward each other? Are there any actions or consequences that arise from this event and, if so, where do they lead the characters?

Because this is such a significant moment in the romantic relationship, take another look at the six-step structure for major turning points earlier in this chapter and be sure to cover each point from this method.

Example
Murder Most Unusual (Michelle Somers)

Long version
Stacey approaches Chase for research on her award-winning novel. Her idea of authenticity is re-enacting murders at real crime scenes with a mannequin as a victim. Chase sees her as a little wacky and a whole lot sexy, but harmless. He fights the attraction, refusing to start something he may not be around to finish.

Eighteen months later, with her book's notoriety, Chase realizes he missed something in the original investigation – the serial killer *terrorizing Melbourne is using Stacey's stories as his blueprint for murder. As she writes the sequel, dead bodies litter her path. When Chase questions her, he gleans nothing but an overwhelming hunger to steal a kiss. Desire and the need to **feel** forgoes sense and he does just that, until reality slams him with a chilling thought: is this irresistible fruit-loop a cold-blooded killer?*

*Stacey can't stop thinking about **that** kiss. She'd imagined kissing the hunky detective, so like the heroes in her books, but imaginings had nothing on the real, hot, wondrous reality. Despite her distracting thoughts, Stacey has a scene to enact, which means a trip to a fishing superstore for supplies. She turns around and there is Chase. Again. Stalking her. She's not wrong, but her assumptions about his reasons are off. Still, she bowls in, foot-in-mouth, declaring that his interest is a waste of time as she doesn't date. His laughter follows her home, along with questions about her movements a particular day eighteen months ago. Why'd he mention it?* (**248** words)

Short version

Chase helps Stacey with writing-related research. Her idea of authenticity is re-enacting murders with a mannequin victim. Sure, she's a little wacky and a whole lot sexy, but harmless. He fights the attraction, refusing to start something he may not be around to finish.

*Then Stacey's novel wins an award and Chase realizes his initial investigation missed something – the killer terrorizing Melbourne is mimicking Stacey's murders. As she writes the sequel, dead bodies litter her path. Chase questions her, gleaning nothing but an overwhelming hunger to steal a kiss. The need to **feel** forgoes sense and he succumbs, until a chilling reality slams him: is this irresistible fruit-loop a cold-blooded killer?*

*Stacey can't forget **that** kiss. Despite her distracting thoughts, she has a scene to enact. She visits a fishing superstore only to find Chase there. Stalking her. She bowls in, foot-in-mouth, declaring he's wasting his time – she doesn't date. His laughter follows her home, along with questions about a day eighteen months ago. Why'd he mention it?* (168 words)

There you have it – two information-packed paragraphs from my second novel, *Murder Most Unusual*. These two versions are great examples of how you can manipulate the content of your synopsis. Let's break them down and see what information I've managed to include.

From the orienting paragraphs, we know that Chase is a homicide detective who believes he's inherited the disease that killed his mother. And we know that Stacey is a romantic suspense author who believes love is as fictional as her stories. Her ex-husband helped with that.

We know how they feel about each other before the kiss. Chase is attracted to Stacey. He thinks she's a fruit-loop, but harmless. Stacey has imagined kissing the man so like the heroes she writes, but their kiss was better than anything she's written.

After the kiss, Chase pulls away, questioning whether Stacey is responsible for the murders. Stacey refuses to be distracted from what matters – her book. Plus, she doesn't date, so there's no room in her life for Chase, or any man for that matter. Not after the disaster that was her marriage. So we know their feelings before and after.

What do they plan to do? Chase is already doing it: questioning Stacey to see what she knows – if anything – about the murders. And Stacey? Well, she's planning the next scene for her book. Although, that last sentence suggests she may try to discover why a particular date is of interest to Chase.

Bear in mind that you don't have to answer each of these questions directly. Yes, in a synopsis we 'tell' instead of 'showing', but by using subtext and showing the way a character acts or reacts, it's possible to reveal how a character feels or doesn't feel without spelling it out. For example, if a character makes jokes or deflects in emotional situations, this shows a tendency toward denying their feelings.

Let's take a closer look at these paragraphs to make sure they pass the six-step structure for major turning points test.

Plot

» *What plot point led to this event taking place?*
Chase realizes a series of murders in Melbourne matches the murders in Stacey's book. He questions Stacey, then attraction takes hold and he kisses her.

» *What goal does this relate to?*
Chase wants a future he doesn't believe he'll have. Kissing Stacey makes him *feel*, something he usually refuses to do, because feeling highlights the emptiness in his life.

Character

» *Who is driving this plot point?*
Chase – he kisses Stacey.

Action

» *What action do they take as a result of this plot point?*
Chase pulls back when he considers she could be a killer. Then he tails her to see what she does. Stacey pushes the kiss from her mind and determinedly focuses on planning her next scene by going to a store and buying supplies. She thinks Chase is following her because he's interested romantically, so she tells him he's wasting his time. Then as an afterthought, she wonders why he asks her about a particular date.

Motivation

» *What motivated the action?*
Desire and Chase's need to *feel*. Something he doesn't

normally allow himself, because he doesn't believe he has a future. As for Stacey backing away, she doesn't want a relationship and she doesn't need a man in her life. Been there, done that, she won't revisit that rocky road again.

Reaction

» *How does the instigator feel during? After? What are their thoughts?*
Chase feels conflicted. He wants to continue kissing Stacey, but passion-killer of passion-killers – she might just be a murderer. With this thought, Chase reverts to detective-mode, a mechanical non-emotional place where he doesn't have to feel.

» *How does the receiver react to this action?*
Stacey is stunned, turned on and angry – she pushes Chase away by telling him she's not interested.

» *How do they feel? Show emotion?*
Stacey hates that she liked the kiss, hates that Chase treats her as if she's a joke. Not much different to her ex-husband (mentioned in the orienting paragraphs). She hides her emotions, denies she's interested. Not dating, not letting a man in, is her way of protecting her heart.

Impact

» *What impact or change does this action have on their ongoing relationship?*
Chase is determined to stick to work and the case, and forget that his kiss with a possible killer has made him feel. Stacey storms off, telling Chase his interest is a waste of time: she doesn't date and has no intention of changing.

Of course, I could delve deeper into this scene with a longer synopsis length; or I could further cut back on words and descriptions if something shorter was required. Once I have the bare bones of my turning points, I can craft each paragraph according to need. Just remember that old mantra – you can't edit an empty page. So, write your synopsis, include what you believe to be necessary, and then slowly carve back or expand, depending on the requirements of the submission guidelines.

Your turn . . .

Choose a movie or book you love and write a first kiss paragraph. Or write one for your current work in progress.

Remember, this is a pivotal moment in your central characters' budding relationship and more than likely the first time they get up close and personal in your story. Make sure you do the moment justice. Inject emotion and tension into your writing and don't forget to apply the six-step structure for major turning points: plot, character, action, motivation, reaction and impact.

FIRST KISS BREAKDOWN

PLOT:

CHARACTER:

ACTION:

MOTIVATION:

REACTION:

IMPACT:

FIRST KISS PARAGRAPH

3. SUBSEQUENT TURNING POINTS

As mentioned previously, these turning points are major events or scenes that mark a change in your central characters' relationship. They include:

» First sparks of trust.
» First or pivotal heart's talk.
» First time they make love.
» Any major, pivotal shift in their relationship.
» Any major 'aha!' moment in relation to their goals and/or their relationship.
» Any major stuff-ups – times they get things wrong or stumble – that set them back in terms of their goals and/or the relationship.

These turning points comprise critical moments in a romance, yet most writers tend to overlook them when crafting their synopsis. Examples include heart-to-heart exchanges, moments of intimacy, revelations blurted out in the heat of the moment or whispered in the wilds of passion, or perhaps a point in time when the central characters had their chance to reveal something and didn't, leading to disaster. Instants that all earn a place here if they've exerted a direct impact on the developing relationship of your central characters.

Make sure when you include these events that you provide a snapshot of before-and-after. How do the characters view each other before the event? How do they feel? Then, as the event takes place, once again analyze their emotions. How are they changing? How do they feel and react after the event? And what is the impact of this event on their relationship?

If your story sits outside of the romance genre, include turning points that are closely linked to your central theme or that relate to either story or character arc. Any event that drives or hinders the plot and/or character growth requires a mention. Any major, life-changing decisions or changes in the course of events must also be included to provide a clear and full picture of your protagonist's journey, both internal and external, and a natural progression toward their new world as depicted in your concluding paragraphs.

It's a lot to take in, I know. So let's have a look at how to put it all into practice.

Example
Worth the Risk (Michelle Somers)

We've met Alise and Colt (nee Darius) in Chapter 2: Central characters. We know that Alise and Darius were friends in high school until Alise suspected Darius of selling marijuana to the boy who killed her sister. Ten years later she meets Colt, Darius's celebrity persona, and fails to recognize the boy she once knew. Not surprising, since he's traded his glasses and geeky persona for contact lenses, muscles and a tan. Then after a one-night stand and a moment she dreamily wishes could become more, Alise discovers his true identity. A devastating mix of furious, hurt and betrayed, she storms off, vowing never to forgive him.

Now we arrive at a pivotal scene. Alise is in the offices of Blues Away – a mental health support service – for an interview on her life beyond depression. Darius just happens to be in there on business – deliberately. He's hoping to run into her.

When gunshots ring out and everyone but Alise evacuates, Darius rushes back into the building to save her. This is what happens after he finds her:

Darius leads Alise to an iron door, types in a code and bundles them both inside a high-security storeroom. It seems Darius Fraser has more to explain than his duplicity of the past week.

They barricade the door and through an outpouring of hurt and accusations, their barriers crumble. Darius reveals he's the silent founder of Blues Away, stunning Alise, challenging her preconceptions about the man who lied and the boy who betrayed her. How can someone so bad do something so selfless? They begin an exchange of yo-yo confessions, leading to that fateful event their graduation year, the moment when misconceptions killed their friendship and carved their disparate futures.

Alise shares the story behind her sister's death, that she reported Darius to the police because she believed he and the drugs were to blame. Darius reveals he pretended the drugs were his to cover for his wayward brother, keeping him safe, fulfilling a promise to his dying father. Alise is shocked and filled with regret. With an adult's reasoning, she sees Darius wasn't to blame. For the first time in ten years Darius understands Alise's overreaction, and he forgives. Old feelings resurface and amidst fears they may not escape their confines alive, heat flares, passion seizes and they make love, repairing the past and sealing the future.

With shock, Darius realizes he never stopped loving Alise, that his feelings were buried all this time beneath the hurt of her perceived betrayal. Alise discovers that beneath the famous model exterior, Darius is still the same boy who became her friend back in school, the boy she thought she was falling in love with until a crack in her life-line caused her destiny to swerve.

Heavy stuff, right?

So, there we have it. A complex example, I'll admit, but all the better to demonstrate how much or little information is necessary to inject clarity into a scene. Can you see the fundamental role this event plays in the repair of Alise and Darius's relationship? It's a huge turning point; a major 'aha' moment for both characters; a moment of understanding and discovery where the misconceptions of youth and the past have been stripped away, leaving a realization of lost opportunities and a chance to try again.

In contrast, there are moments when a character should come clean, but doesn't. How important are they?

Disney's *Aladdin*

With the help of a genie and a single wish, street urchin Aladdin has transformed into Prince Ali – a man worthy of living in a palace and marrying a princess. He has just spent a magical night with Princess Jasmine, journeying the world on the flying carpet, and then this happens:

> *Head in the clouds, Aladdin leaves Jasmine only to be set upon by Jafar's guards. They tie him up and toss him into a lake, forcing him to use his second wish to escape. Outraged, he returns to the palace just in time to stop Jafar from hypnotizing the sultan into giving him Jasmine's hand in marriage. Aladdin breaks the spell and Jafar vanishes. Jasmine rushes into Aladdin's arms. Ecstatic his daughter has finally found love, the sultan gives his blessing for marriage. Giddy with happiness, Jasmine pulls Aladdin aside, stunning him with the news that after they are married he will be sultan and rule Agrabah.*

> *Aladdin is torn. The finery, the lamp, the lies – none of it makes him a real prince worthy of a princess. But no matter how much the genie pleads, freeing him and telling Jasmine the truth is not an option – he won't risk losing everything he's come to love.*

This is a great example of a turning point that leads a character to a moment of truth. Aladdin has always believed life as a prince – living in a palace – was the answer to all his troubles, and he's dreamed of living there for as long as he can remember. And now, of course, there's that added incentive of marrying the princess.

However, there's a harsh reality attached to that dream: he'll become sultan and will be responsible for the city and people of Agrabah. This reality sparks a moment of self-assessment where

Aladdin finds himself lacking, and he's hit with the weight of his lies. Yet, he's not ready to come clean. He still wants the dream, much as its sparkle is beginning to fade.

It's here that a crack appears in Aladdin's goal. And it's this critical incident that leads to the next critical turning point – the black moment.

Your turn . . .

Before we visit the black moment, why not have a go at crafting a few more turning point paragraphs.

Analyze your current work in progress, or an old manuscript you're considering revisiting. What major turning points can you identify? Are there any 'aha' moments? Character revelations? Emotion-packed heart-to-heart exchanges? Have either of the characters uncovered something personal about their counterpart? Has some plot event occurred that pushes the couple closer together? Or encourages a higher level of trust? Or forces them to question their goals, their life's direction, the way they view the other character?

See how many of these points you can list for your story, and then build the paragraphs using the six-step structure for major turning points. Make sure you cover all six steps: plot, character, action, motivation, reaction and impact.

TURNING POINT BREAKDOWN

PLOT:

CHARACTER:

ACTION:

MOTIVATION:

REACTION:

IMPACT:

TURNING POINT PARAGRAPH

4. THE BLACK MOMENT

This is the instant in your story when all seems lost. In romance, it's the moment when the reader wonders how your central characters – the almost happy couple – will ever scale this obstacle to find their happy ever after.

So, how does the black moment unfold? To begin with, the central characters are happy, comfortable, together. Things seem almost perfect. They have what they think they want. This doesn't necessarily equate to what will make them happy, but it's an intrinsic part of their GMC.

There are still some unresolved conflicts, still a little more of their character arc to scale, but they are content – or at least they tell themselves they are content – to push these aside and enjoy their new-found affinity and closeness. For example, they may believe they want a no-strings relationship with their counterpart, and they win it. They are happy, yet they feel something is missing. Instead of listening to the niggle in their subconscious, they push it aside and determine to enjoy what they've got. After all, it was what they wanted, right?

Then a grenade surfaces and someone pulls the pin. The moment of disaster – the black moment – when whatever happiness and affinity they've shared is ripped out from under them. At this stage of your synopsis, it is important to accentuate the contrast between the moments before and the moments after disaster hits.

Example
Lethal in Love (Michelle Somers)

I have to confess that I've adjusted these paragraphs to avoid spoilers. This is not the original synopsis I used for my submission to Penguin Random House. After all, I'd hate you to come to this moment in *Lethal in Love* and guess the ending.

With this example, I want to demonstrate how to build up to the black moment, before tearing everything back down, devastating your central characters to a point where everything seems lost.

My central characters are Jayda, a homicide detective, and Seth, a reporter. Circumstances have thrown them into working together to catch the Night Terror – a serial killer who is terrorizing young women in Melbourne, Australia. For the better part of this story, the Night Terror has been closing in on Jayda. Bit by agonizing bit, he's stolen all sense of her security and confidence. None of her close family or friends are who they seem. Everyone is hiding something. Everyone is suspect. Everyone but Seth. He is the only one she feels she can trust, and she turns to him. For comfort. For support. For love.

Then *wham!*

Take a look and see how I've structured this section which spans from making progress, higher stakes and all is lost to the black moment:

> *As they uncover each new clue together, Jayda and Seth find more than physical comfort in each other's arms. Seth talks about his parents and his need to prove he's not a failure. Jayda confides her disappointment over her parents' split. She talks about her sister, their relationship and growing up together. They discover an affinity they never believed could exist.*
>
> *Then the lab contacts Jayda with a DNA match from the last murder scene – a man by the name of James Allen.*
>
> *A man who happens to be her twin brother. And the Night Terror.*
>
> *Jayda's world tumbles – her life is a lie. She confronts her adoptive father and he tells her the truth.[1] Now, it's a race to find the real killer before police discover their blood ties. Unbeknownst to Jayda, her twin is deeply ensconced in her new life as a close family friend, his every step targeted toward destroying her and her happiness.*

---

1 *'the truth' her father shares here was already outlined in Jayda's orienting paragraph as part of her GMC. There's no need to repeat it again.*

Jayda finds comfort in Seth's arms. And he finds – uncharacteristically – a burning need to be there for her. When they make love, Jayda is shocked to discover that's exactly what it is—love. She's found what she believed didn't exist. The promise of a life past all the craziness breathes hope and joy into her heart.

Waking early, she opens Seth's laptop to begin the online search for her sibling, only to discover Seth's secret – his news-breaking story is the story of her life. Devastated, Jayda runs to her family friend. As she stares at the family portrait on his wall, the reason it always sent shivers down her spine becomes clear: it belongs to her nightmarish past.

It's important to note here that some romance subgenres may contain two distinct black moments – one for the romance and one for the plot. Even though they may occur separately, these two events are often closely linked, where one event triggers the other.

In the previous example, I covered the romantic black moment. But what of the plot black moment? It followed closely in the next paragraph:

*As the realization hits, so does a heavy **thud**! against her skull. When Jayda awakens, she is cuffed to a pipe in an old warehouse. And her brother is watching.*

This addition is short, sharp and to the point. I haven't delved into great detail for this turning point, the synopsis doesn't require it. But I have delivered this event in a fresh and interesting way, while injecting the moment with suspense.

So, there we have it – a partial rewrite of my original *Lethal in Love* synopsis. Do you see how we *feel* Jayda and Seth's connection? How we witness their growing closeness, how we *believe* it. This is vitally important. Not only should we believe the connection between your central characters in your story, but we must believe it in your synopsis as well. If you haven't shown their growing relationship, if you haven't included those vital plot points that lead them to a deeper trust and feeling, if we don't experience their emotion and their growing need for each other, when we arrive at the black moment, we won't experience the full extent of their loss, their betrayal, their devastation. Then, and only then, are you able to move out from the billowing cloud that is the black moment to the next portion of your story: that wonderful, heart-warming sigh that is the resolution. But before we move onto that portion of your synopsis . . .

Your turn . . .

What are some classic black moments? Think of a movie or book you've read recently, or create a black moment of your own. Perhaps consider your current work in progress and write a turning-point paragraph for the moment the world crashes in and all seems lost. Take a close look and identify whether there are multiple black moments, maybe one for the plot and one for the romance? See if you can create a paragraph encompassing both.

Make sure you craft your black moment paragraph using the six-step structure for major turning points. Make sure you cover all six steps: plot, character, action, motivation, reaction and impact.

BLACK MOMENT BREAKDOWN

PLOT:

CHARACTER:

ACTION:

MOTIVATION:

REACTION:

IMPACT:

BLACK MOMENT PARAGRAPH

CHAPTER 4
THE RESOLUTION

This is the fun part of the synopsis. The home straight. The last piece of the puzzle slips into place, your central characters gaze into each other's eyes, and they come together, nothing—absolutely nothing—keeping them apart. Okay, so that's a little cliché, but you get my meaning. This is that wondrous moment just before the happy ever after.

No unresolved tension or conflict should remain at the end of your story; the same can be said for your synopsis. While the synopsis will not include ALL the conflicts in your book, it will contain the main ones. And those should be resolved by this point. Make sure all loose threads – including conflicts, plot twists and problems – have been tied up. Be careful not to tie up those minor threads that didn't make it into your synopsis. It's too easy to perform a wide sweep at this stage, wrapping everything up in a nice tidy bow. This is the place that issues outside of your synopsis might suddenly, magically, appear. And there's nothing more confusing to a reader – a prospective editor or agent – than having a problem solved that they were unaware even existed.

If your story falls outside the romance genre, the resolution paragraph should show how your story concludes, whether that be happily, tragically or bitter-sweet. We will have seen a shift in your central character's life. Where are they at the end of their journey? How have they grown? What have they learned? Gained? Lost? Show how the world they inhabit now differs from their world at the onset of their story.

Again, make sure you keep the six-step structure for major turning points at the forefront of your mind while crafting these paragraphs.

Examples

Lethal in Love (Michelle Somers)

Jayda finally comes face to face with the Night Terror and this is what happens:

> *As years of pent-up resentment pour out of her brother's mouth, Jayda tries to reason with him. Unsuccessfully. He pulls out a knife and approaches, threatening to kill her in the same manner he killed her mother. A gunshot interrupts. He slumps to the ground and Seth is there, freeing her hands, pulling her into his arms, vowing a happy ever after she'd given up all hope of finding.*

This is an altered excerpt from my 1000-word synopsis for *Lethal in Love* and it covers seven chapters of the novel. Yes, *seven* – that's a lot of coverage for less than ten lines. Within those chapters, we see the interaction between Jayda and her captor, and we see this sadistic killer finally meet his sticky end. It's the essence of this that I have to convey in my resolution, nothing more.

By including this example, I want to demonstrate that you don't need to provide the detail from those chapters. I've captured the crux here in this short but succinct paragraph. For the detail, the reader will need to read my manuscript, which just so happens to have been the aim of this synopsis – to impress the targeted editor or agent with my story enough to gain a request.

Games of Seduction (Michelle Somers)

We met Robbie and Marcy earlier, in Chapter 2: Opening paragraphs, Putting a hook into context. This is what happens when Robbie and Marcy finally get together:

> *On a night out with the girls, a friend orders the despondent Marcy to get off her ass, get some gumption and fight for what she*

wants. Whoa! Talk about being thrown. This advice from the last person she'd expected – a poster-board for sex-without-sentiment. Realization slams: if Marcy doesn't change something, she'll end up nowhere but where she is now, heartbroken and lonely. It's time to seize control of her destiny and run with it.

Robbie is suffering through the dinner-disaster from hell. He stares into eyes not amber, surrounded by hair not curls of caramel, and realizes his biggest mistake outside of the date was letting Marcy go. He should have trusted more and given her the opportunity to explain – as he did with his mother.[2]

He rushes to Marcy's apartment only to find it empty. Disheartened, he returns home and finds a familiar form on his front steps – Marcy. A heady mix of hope and relief see him rush toward her. They bare their souls, opening their hearts, wide and willingly. With a declaration of love, Robbie tumbles Marcy into his arms. They fall into bed and inaugurate the beginning of the rest of their lives.

Marcy is ready to trust again. Ready to begin living the rest of her life with Robbie. As their lips meet, her last thoughts are drowned in a sea of sensation and a game of seduction that moves way past the here and now, to forever and after.

Very simplistic, but there we have it. All conflicts have been resolved and we are presented with a conclusion. Not only have both Marcy and Robbie decided they want and need each other above all else, but they've both taken steps to ensure it happens, seeking each other out, ready to do whatever it takes to win the other back.

Did you notice how I linked the opening paragraphs to the resolution? This is a powerful way of rounding up a synopsis. Earlier in the book, we saw Robbie start out with a plan to seduce Marcy, and in the last paragraph there is a reference to his 'game of seduction'. The story

---

2   *This relates to an earlier plot point and is a key motivator in Robbie's GMC*

has come full-circle, but the characters have grown. Conflict has been replaced by contentment and a happy ever after well worth waiting for.

How the Sheriff Was Won (Anne Gracie)

Anne Gracie has graciously provided me with the synopsis for her Harlequin Duets comedy *How the Sheriff Was Won*, and I couldn't resist using her last paragraph, the resolution portion of her story.

This is a gorgeous, humorous tale about a big-city crime reporter and a small-town sheriff. Jassie McQuilty figures she'll stay a year in the small town of Bear Claw, whip the resident Globe newspaper – which also happens to be her inheritance – into shape, and then leave again with a sizeable profit and the title 'managing editor' on her CV.

Sheriff Stone has been burned twice too many times – he won't open himself up for a third. So when Jassie sets him in her sights, for a bout of fun while she wiles away her time in the sticks, he rebuffs her every advance.

The synopsis is as hysterical as the story, with Anne cleverly sprinkling Jassie's news headlines throughout. From '*handsome, virile sheriff foils daylight robbery*' to '*sheriff denies virility claim – Globe to investigate*'.

Look how Anne weaves the story and theme together in this last, marvelous paragraph:

> *Belatedly Jassie realizes that she truly loves Stone. She writes a limited edition of the newspaper (circulation – 1) containing an apology and a declaration of love and sends it to the sheriff's office. Shortly afterwards she reports a doughnut burglary and sends out an SOS to which Stone eagerly responds. They declare their love and all is blissful between them. In bed together the next morning, Stone can see she is planning a new headline. He imagines it's going to be something mushy and romantic about their wedding and asks her for details. She tells him: SHERIFF PROVES VIRILITY QUESTION—GLOBE EDITOR MORE THAN SATISFIED.*

I don't know about you, but reading that paragraph alone makes me want to run out and buy the book. Not only is Anne's synopsis ending 'satisfying', it's funny as well – in true romcom form. It leaves the reader with a warm, fuzzy feeling and a need to know more about these two very different, very appealing characters.

In this example, Anne reiterates my comments on linking opening and closing paragraphs when resolving a story. Show how far your characters have journeyed and how far the romance has developed, and prepare for the next and final portion of your synopsis – the conclusion.

Your turn . . .

Time for you to write a satisfying resolution to your story. Consider the events and circumstances that have kept your central characters apart, and what conflicts need to be resolved so they can commit one hundred percent to each other and their newfound relationship. Then show all this in your resolution paragraph by applying the six-step structure for major turning points. Make sure you match tone, voice and vocabulary to genre. Make your resolution as believable and satisfying in your synopsis as you would in your manuscript. And make it engaging enough to spur the reader, i.e., editor or agent, into requesting a copy of your story in full.

RESOLUTION BREAKDOWN

PLOT:

CHARACTER:

ACTION:

MOTIVATION:

REACTION:

IMPACT:

RESOLUTION PARAGRAPH

CHAPTER 5
CONCLUSION

You're nearly there! This is your final paragraph – unless you have already amalgamated your story's conclusion into your resolution paragraphs. Everything is resolved. There's no conflict. No tension. No threads left untied. Your central characters have found their happy ever after and now all you need is a line or short paragraph showing how the story leaves them in those critical, final pages and beyond.

As I mentioned above, sometimes this will form part of the resolution. Sometimes, especially in the case of an epilogue, it will require its own paragraph. This is particularly important with issues that require a time lapse to show that all is well in the world that is the new couple's romance.

Examples of this might be showing that a fight against illness or disease has been won. The baby your couple never thought they could have is born. A business success or accolade has been reached. Let's take a look at a few examples.

Worth the Risk (Michelle Somers)

In this story, one of Alise's main conflicts was her belief that she couldn't fall pregnant. One of Darius's goals was to create a family resembling the one he never had growing up. This was a big issue for both characters, although when it came to a choice, Darius chose Alise over his dream of a family and Alise chose to trust in Darius's love for her. It was important for me to show how everything worked out for the couple in the end. And this is how I did it, with my resolution paragraphs first, followed by a short, one-sentence conclusion:

> *The doctor appears, and after a brief examination he reveals both Alise and the baby will be just fine.*
>
> *Alise's insides freeze. She can't be pregnant! It's impossible! The doctor assures her she can and it's not, explaining that her condition ten years ago could have been a consequence of her stressful marriage and depression. Darius drops to one knee and proposes, and Alise follows her heart. She can do this, do anything, with Darius by her side.*
>
> *And two years later, married and pregnant again, Alise agrees – love is always worth the risk.*

Notice how I've linked the conclusion to the central theme of the story? How it's often those risks we take in life that pay the biggest dividends; for Alise, leaping into relationship waters again after escaping her disastrous first marriage and the resulting depression; for Darius, opening up and laying his heart bare in the hope he won't be rejected again. And finally, at the culmination of their journey, they both won their happy ever after, as is the way of romance.

Lethal in Love (Michelle Somers)

These two paragraphs encompass the last two-and-a-half chapters of the novel. The Night Terror serial killer is caught, both hero and heroine are safe, and Jayda is in hospital recovering from her injuries.

This is how I chose to round up Jayda and Seth's story:

> *As Seth waits for Jayda to regain consciousness, he vows never to leave her side again.*
>
> *Jayda wakens with thoughts of new beginnings. Seth drops to one knee and her heart fills as he offers her a happy-ever-after she'd given up all hope of finding.*

Satisfying? I hope so. After all this couple has been through – fighting their own personal demons plus fighting the flesh-and-blood 'demon' intent on killing them both – they've earned their happy moment. The reader can breathe a sigh of relief and smile. Exactly the reaction I hope to generate from these two short paragraphs.

Your turn . . .

See if you can write a one or two sentence conclusion for the following scenarios:

- » Unplanned pregnancy
- » Wanted but unexpected pregnancy
- » One character moves countries or states to be with the other
- » Recovery of a sick or injured central character
- » Promotion situation where one central character becomes the supervisor of another

Can you think of any others?

When crafting this sentence or paragraph, don't forget to use your unique voice and tone, while keeping the writing both simple and brief. Imagine how this story might have started and try linking beginning and end and central theme. Show character and/or story arc. Use an economy of words and give a snapshot of the central characters and their state of mind as they enter this happy ever after phase of their lives.

CONCLUSION BREAKDOWN

PLOT:

CHARACTER:

ACTION:

MOTIVATION:

REACTION:

IMPACT:

CONCLUSION PARAGRAPH

And there ends your synopsis – hopefully not as painful as you'd once imagined.

Let's review what we've covered so far. What should you see when you skim back over your synopsis?

1. Orientation paragraphs comprising your hook, world-building, central theme and central characters.
2. Major turning point paragraphs mapping plot, romance and character arc using the six-step structure for major turning points. Make sure each turning point paragraph covers all six steps: plot, character, action, motivation, reaction and impact.
3. Resolution paragraph resolving all conflicts and tying up all loose ends, leaving both central characters and readers fully satisfied.
4. Conclusion line or paragraph showing the contented couple ready to embark on their happy ever after or happy for now.

Congratulations! You've gathered your content and, brick-by-brick, laid the framework for a stellar synopsis. And you're almost done. There are just a few additional points to cover before you can sigh with relief and hit 'send' on your submission.

The first of those additional points? Backstory. How do we demonstrate the impact of the past on the present without confusing the reader and tangling our synopsis in a web of excessive detail?

CHAPTER 6
BACKSTORY

Backstory is an event or events that have occurred prior to the beginning of your story. For most of us, the term 'backstory' is interminably linked to words like 'info dump' or, more accurately, 'avoid info dump'.

Of course, backstory is important. It's a huge motivator for our characters. It explains why they act and feel the way they do on each and every page. Without revealing a character's backstory, their actions or reactions to a seemingly harmless event can appear completely out of context. Or hugely over-reactive.

So we need backstory, but how much? We're taught when writing to thread backstory in 'only as it becomes relevant', and only as much as is required at the time to make the action or reaction make sense. We're told not to dump huge chunks of backstory into the beginning of our novel. It's boring, distracting and will only pull the reader out of the narrative with no guarantee they'll ever drop themselves back in. In short, backstory doesn't belong in the beginning of a novel.

Does the same rule apply to a synopsis? In my opinion, not always. We introduce our central characters in the first couple of paragraphs of the synopsis. As part of this we introduce their GMC, of which backstory plays a huge part. The events in a character's past shape the person they are today and can form the basis of their motivation and conflict. These factors need to be introduced upfront, clearly and concisely, in your synopsis.

For example, if your heroine is wary of men because a series of males has let her down in the past – her father, her brother, her best friend, her husband or any combination of these and others – then we need to know. This feeds into her character, providing justification and reason for her distrust of, let's say, a gorgeous, gentle but overly persistent hero.

How do we keep backstory to a minimum? Pick out the key points – the ones your story won't make sense without. Then weave them into one complex sentence or combine several sentences until you've provided the information your reader needs to understand your characters.

Example

Worth the Risk (Michelle Somers)

It's three years since ALISE RIERDAN's divorce from a control-freak and the resulting depression. Ten since her high-school friend and prom date sold drugs to the man who killed her sister. Relationships with men she doesn't want or need, unless they're the fleeting kind. So, it's time for fun and experiences missed in her youth – the ever-elusive orgasm and a sexy man to deliver it. If only she knew where to look and wasn't so tongue-glued-to-roof-of-mouth shy when she found him.

DARIUS FRASER has clawed his way out of mediocrity and the foster-care system that contained him. A bespectacled nerd turned international model, he seldom thinks back to the girl who trampled his heart and destroyed his dreams of scholarship by reporting him to the cops for a crime he didn't commit. Because of her, he failed his promise to his dying father – to look after his mentally ill mother and keep his younger brother from harm. Now, he wants more than anything to recreate the family he once had. To find that one special woman to fill the void in his empty fame-filled life.

Within these two detail-packed paragraphs we get a sense of Alise and Darius's joined history, their goals, their motivations and their conflicts. We don't have an entire narrative of backstory, we have merely a hint, just enough to put these characters and their GMCs into context; just enough to establish the conflict that will flare between them when they reacquaint on the page, but not so much that we waste valuable words and drown the reader in events that happened way before our story even started.

In contrast, sometimes backstory events require a mention in our synopsis, but not in the opening paragraphs. In these cases, we can weave the reference into the body of the synopsis, positioning it where it most makes sense.

Let's take a look at how this transpires in practice:

Lethal in Love (Michelle Somers)

This hint of backstory occurs seven paragraphs into the synopsis, at a point where homicide detective, Jayda, is contemplating teaming up with reporter, Seth, to catch the Night Terror serial killer.

> *Past experience proves reporters are ruthless and unscrupulous. But Jayda will make a deal with the devil if it means finding the killer.*

In very few words, I've given context to Jayda's hostile reaction toward Seth, and reporters in general. Somewhere in her past, Jayda has crossed paths with one or more reporters, and they've tainted her view on the entire profession. We don't need to know the particulars of these interactions; it's enough to know they exist. Leave the details for your manuscript.

Murder Most Unusual (Michelle Somers)

Once again, this excerpt is seven paragraphs into the synopsis.

> *Cops are a pain in Stacey's ass. Cops like her father who hide behind a stream of humor and drink themselves into oblivion. That happy-go-lucky façade won't suck her into thinking the person behind it was basically good and honest and worthy of her love. Her mother cottoned on and broke away from her father—and the experience left her bitter and controlling. Stacey won't follow down that same road.*

Again, we are given context. Stacey's anti-cop stance is deeply ingrained into her psyche as a result of her past. Her father quite categorically saw to that. Yet, she writes sexy cop stories. Who knows why? Perhaps her stories represent the kind of men she wished her father had been. A little Freudian, but something to think about nevertheless . . .

In summary, backstory falls into two distinct categories:

1. Events that impact directly on the central characters' GMCs

These events are intrinsic to a character's motivation and/or conflict. They explain what is driving them in search of their goal, and they often demonstrate why the two central characters cannot be together at the onset of your story.

Examples include bad experiences with the opposite sex that may jade a character's view on relationships; bullying or abuse that makes them withdrawn and antisocial, or cold, unemotional and detached; loss of family or loved ones driving them to build a new circle of people – like a band of security – around them, or it may have the opposite effect, where they go to the extreme of avoiding close relationships so they never experience the associated feelings of hurt and abandonment again.

2. Events that elicit specific emotions or overreactions in our central characters

These events spark specific reactions from our characters – either physical or emotional – that can impact on their behavior in relation to major turning points. These events should be woven into the body of a synopsis only if they are required to make sense of a stance or situation.

Examples include a character's bad experience with a particular profession – for example, police officers, reporters, lawyers or doctors – that would explain dislike or distrust; avoidance of particular situations or places – for example, hospitals, a particular landmark, their childhood home – due to bad memories; learned fears or phobias from childhood family and/or friends or from personal past bad experiences – for example, fear of dogs, phobia of heights or enclosed spaces.

Any backstory, regardless the source, is fundamental to building all-rounded characters and all-rounded GMCs. Without these significant events and experiences, your characters will have no motivation to act or react to the provocations you throw their way. There will be no depth to their character and/or their GMC, and nothing to drive their character arc, to change or make a difference in their lives.

All rock-solid reasons to not only ensure we've molded and developed our characters to their full potential on every page of our novel, but to ensure we represent them fully when it comes to our synopsis.

Your turn . . .

What backstories can you create to drive characters with these goals?

- » Determined to be the best in their chosen field.
- » Obsessed about starting a family before they reach the age of twenty-five.
- » Consumed with the need to buy their own home and put every cent they earn into paying off the debt.
- » Crave solitude and security.
- » Need to be out, social and busy, surrounded by people all the time.

What are possible past scenarios that could lead to a character's . . . ?

- » Fear of being alone.
- » Fear of driving.
- » Lack of anything personal in both home and working space.
- » Avoidance of putting down roots and staying in one place for too long.
- » Decision never to have kids.
- » Constant need to be in the limelight.
- » Aversion to members of the opposite sex.

Can you think of any other examples of character goals and their underlying backstories?

CHAPTER 7
SYNOPSIS STRUCTURE
SUMMARY FLOW CHART

Now we've covered the vital components that comprise a stellar synopsis, let's tie all four elements together in a visual overview using the story, Disney's *Aladdin*.

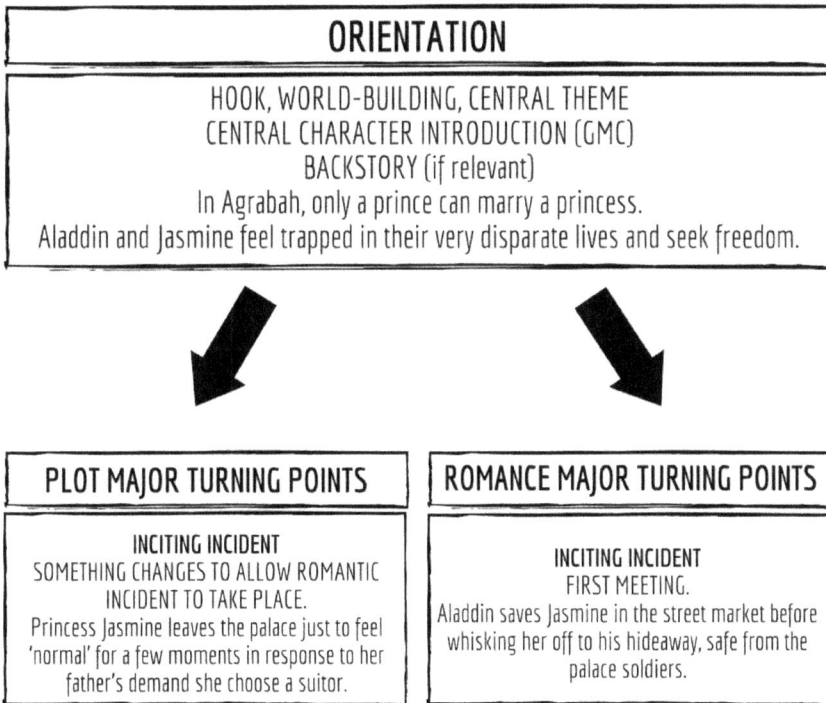

ORIENTATION

HOOK, WORLD-BUILDING, CENTRAL THEME
CENTRAL CHARACTER INTRODUCTION (GMC)
BACKSTORY (if relevant)
In Agrabah, only a prince can marry a princess.
Aladdin and Jasmine feel trapped in their very disparate lives and seek freedom.

PLOT MAJOR TURNING POINTS

INCITING INCIDENT
SOMETHING CHANGES TO ALLOW ROMANTIC INCIDENT TO TAKE PLACE.
Princess Jasmine leaves the palace just to feel 'normal' for a few moments in response to her father's demand she choose a suitor.

ROMANCE MAJOR TURNING POINTS

INCITING INCIDENT
FIRST MEETING.
Aladdin saves Jasmine in the street market before whisking her off to his hideaway, safe from the palace soldiers.

OPPORTUNITY KNOCKS
OPPORTUNITIES ARISE THAT MAKE THE GOAL POSSIBLE.
Aladdin finds a lamp and rubs it, freeing a genie. He escapes the cave with the magic carpet, the genie and three wishes still intact.

OPPORTUNITY KNOCKS
A WAY IS SEEN PAST THE CONFLICTS AND OBSTACLES BLOCKING THE GOAL. FIRST STEPS ARE TAKEN TOWARD ACHIEVEMENT.
Aladdin enters the Cave of Wonders in search of riches that will make him a worthy match for a princess.

MAKING PROGRESS
CHARACTER GRABS CONTROL OF THEIR DESTINY AND JUMPS INTO THE 'MISSION' WITH BOTH FEET. GOAL IS GETTING CLOSER.
Aladdin wishes to be a prince and enters Agrabah in a procession, putting himself forward as a suitor for marriage to the princess.

MAKING PROGRESS
TENSION IS BUILDING. THINGS LOOK LIKE THEY'RE COMING TOGETHER.
Aladdin takes Jasmine on a carpet ride and they share their first kiss.

NO TURNING BACK NOW
PERSONALLY INVESTED. COULDN'T TURN BACK EVEN IF THEY WANTED TO.
After being grabbed by the royal guards, Aladdin escapes and enters the palace in time to free the sultan from Jafar's spell. Jafar escapes.

NO TURNING BACK NOW
EMOTIONALLY INVESTED.
The sultan sees how in love Aladdin and Jasmine are and gives his blessing for their marriage.

HIGHER STAKES
THEY HAVE SOMETHING TO LOSE IF THEY FAIL AT THIS POINT.
Jasmine tells Aladdin he will be sultan and rule Agrabah after their marriage.
Aladdin panics. He can't free the genie as he originally promised. He still needs him to continue with his deception.

HIGHER STAKES
THEY ARE BECOMING INVESTED IN EACH OTHER. CONFIDENCES ARE EXCHANGED, FEELINGS ARE DEVELOPING. THERE IS MUCH TO LOSE IF THEY WALK AWAY NOW, INCLUDING THEIR HEARTS.
Aladdin's lies have taken on a life of their own and he can't take them back. He's won the princess, but he'll lose her if he comes clean and reveals he's not really a prince.

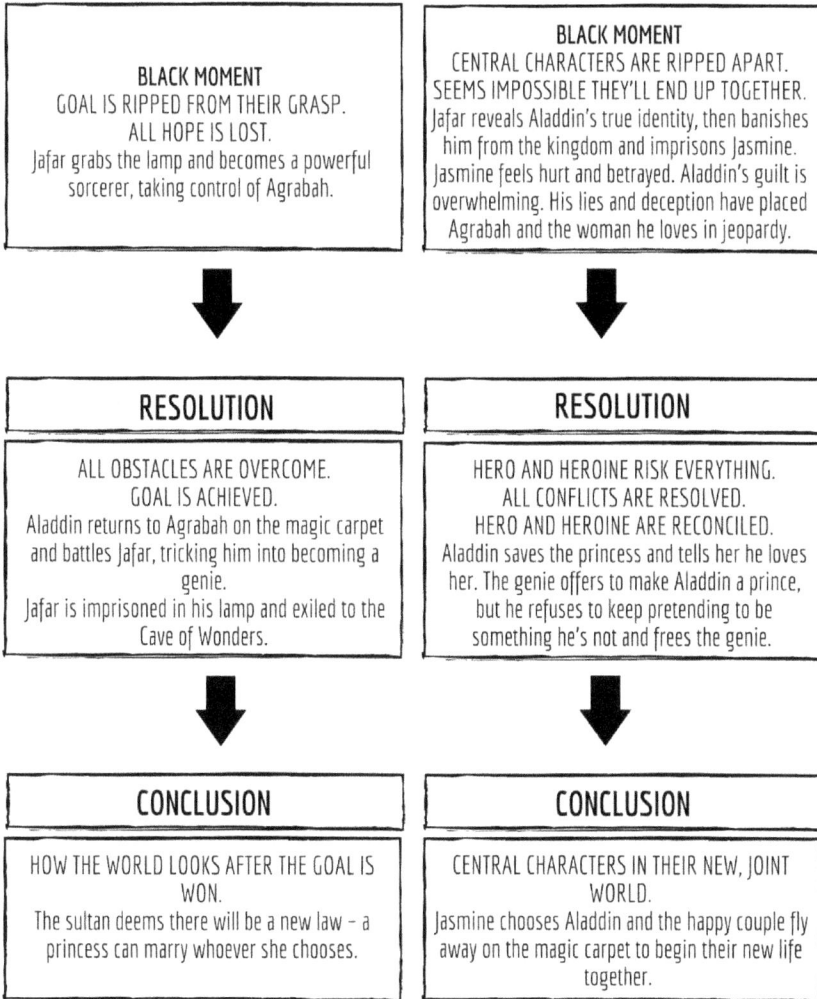

BLACK MOMENT
GOAL IS RIPPED FROM THEIR GRASP.
ALL HOPE IS LOST.
Jafar grabs the lamp and becomes a powerful sorcerer, taking control of Agrabah.

BLACK MOMENT
CENTRAL CHARACTERS ARE RIPPED APART.
SEEMS IMPOSSIBLE THEY'LL END UP TOGETHER.
Jafar reveals Aladdin's true identity, then banishes him from the kingdom and imprisons Jasmine. Jasmine feels hurt and betrayed. Aladdin's guilt is overwhelming. His lies and deception have placed Agrabah and the woman he loves in jeopardy.

RESOLUTION

ALL OBSTACLES ARE OVERCOME.
GOAL IS ACHIEVED.
Aladdin returns to Agrabah on the magic carpet and battles Jafar, tricking him into becoming a genie.
Jafar is imprisoned in his lamp and exiled to the Cave of Wonders.

RESOLUTION

HERO AND HEROINE RISK EVERYTHING.
ALL CONFLICTS ARE RESOLVED.
HERO AND HEROINE ARE RECONCILED.
Aladdin saves the princess and tells her he loves her. The genie offers to make Aladdin a prince, but he refuses to keep pretending to be something he's not and frees the genie.

CONCLUSION

HOW THE WORLD LOOKS AFTER THE GOAL IS WON.
The sultan deems there will be a new law – a princess can marry whoever she chooses.

CONCLUSION

CENTRAL CHARACTERS IN THEIR NEW, JOINT WORLD.
Jasmine chooses Aladdin and the happy couple fly away on the magic carpet to begin their new life together.

And there it is – a method for breaking down your story and building it back up into your synopsis. For writers who are more visual, I hope this chart has taken you that last step toward consolidation and helped you fit all the pieces into the puzzle.

Whichever way you choose to craft your synopsis, whether it be via lists, bullet points or flow charts, always bear in mind the four key elements – orientation, major turning points, resolution, conclusion. Aim for brevity and simplicity. Mention backstory only when and if it is relevant and match tone, voice and vocabulary to genre.

Stay true to the *Simply Synopsis* structure and you'll find at the end of your crafting you will have included all those details and events that are essential to selling and promoting your story.

By closely following the method outlined in these first seven chapters, you will have the makings of a good synopsis. There are a few remaining steps to transform that good synopsis into a great one.

Let's take a closer look at how to tighten and refine and make your synopsis sparkle.

CHAPTER 8
REFINING YOUR SYNOPSIS

Now you've teased out the bare bones of your synopsis, what are the finer points to keep in mind while putting it all together? I may have touched on some of these earlier, but I believe they're important enough to warrant another mention in their very own section.

Voice

A synopsis is a representation of your story, but also your talent as a writer. With a well-crafted synopsis, not only will you show a clear understanding of what makes a great story, but you will provide a taste of your wonderful voice while giving the reader a preview of what they can expect when they sit down and read your book.

» Voice is what makes your manuscript shine.
» Without a great plot and characters you won't have a great story; but without a clear and fresh voice, you'll be left with nothing more than an outline – a list of plot points which are dry, dusty and decidedly dull.
» Your voice is distinctive and wholly yours. It captivates the reader and is one of the key elements drawing them back to your stories, time and time again.
» It's your own unique way of storytelling and a great selling point, because only you can tell a story like you.

Which leads us to the point I'm very long-windedly trekking toward:

» Don't shortchange your synopsis by masking your voice.

» Give your synopsis the same unique qualities you've given your manuscript. Make it fresh, appealing and wholly riveting – a direct reflection of your story.
» Let your voice shine through and draw the reader in, telling your story in a way that's enjoyable and engaging, holding their interest until the very last word.

Tone

Matching tone to genre is enormously important. Make sure your hook – your entire synopsis for that matter – maintains the tone of the genre. Remember, it's a story of your story; a representation of your world, your characters and their lives from their viewpoint.

If your story is a romcom, ensure the humor comes through. If it's a suspense or thriller, make your synopsis chilling. If your story is young adult, don't use words that are 'too old' for that genre. If your story is an historical, don't use modern-day language or descriptions you'd never use in your story; use language and tone to reflect the era.

For example, if your story is set in a time without rotary washing machines, don't refer to them, even in passing, even as part of a simile or metaphor or some form of narrative witticism. A statement such as 'her mind spun tumble-drier fast' doesn't belong anywhere near the manuscript or synopsis of a story set pre-1850s.

Give your synopsis atmosphere and that x-factor you injected into your manuscript. Make it as interesting to read, and as enjoyable, as your story.

Example 1

The Finn Factor (Rachel Bailey)

Genre—New Adult Romance

Sometimes all a girl needs is a little practice . . .

It's been twelve months, three days, and eleven hours since accounting student Scarlett Logan made it past a second date.

Clearly someone needs to teach her how to kiss properly. Like, say, her best friend and roomie, Finn Mackenzie. He's safe, he's convenient, and yeah, maybe just a little gorgeous.

For those who are foreign to new adult romance, this is a set of stories that bridge the gap between the young adult and adult genres. New adult stories tend to focus on issues experienced by characters caught in the years between adolescence and 'true' adulthood, with ages ranging between eighteen to twenty-six years. Issues such as leaving home for the first time, attending college or university, getting that first job, and of course – as the author of this synopsis so beautifully demonstrated in the opening lines – first time love.

Examine the language used here. The pace and tone. The voice. These are all tailored to appeal to eighteen to twenty-six year olds. As we read, we are immediately dropped into Scarlett's world and her generation. And we want to know more.

A synopsis is NOT an outline.

This means a synopsis is *not* a dry recount of plot points; it is a story of your story, and should be written as such. This is the reason why voice and tone are so important. If you build your synopsis around a list of actions and tedious 'and then . . .' openers, you'll fail to capture the interest or imagination of the reader. If your synopsis is dreary, it provides little incentive for an editor or agent to read your story, which just so happens to be your main objective.

So, make your synopsis sparkle, make the story leap from the pages and make it irresistible, riveting reading.

Secondary characters

Only include secondary characters as far as they impact on the development of plot or romance. If you refer to a secondary character in your synopsis, don't use their name. As soon as a name appears in a synopsis, the assumption follows that this character is a central one. Instead, label them by referring to the role they play in relation to your central characters. For example, older sister, mother, boss, old lady next door etc. I'm sure you get the picture.

Remember, your synopsis is a pared-back summary of your plot. Including characters other than your central characters will only bog it down and confuse the reader.

Secondary plots

Secondary plots or stories don't belong in your synopsis. Only include secondary plot points if they have a direct impact on your central plot or characters. And even then, decide whether this is a major or a minor impact. If your synopsis makes sense without your secondary plot, leave it out; otherwise you will muddy the story and confuse the reader – not something you want to do if your aim is to sell your manuscript to an editor or agent.

Explanations of central theme or message

These do not belong in your synopsis. Yes, you want to hint at your story's high concept. What you don't want to do is expound any virtues or morals that your story may address.

A synopsis is not a piece of persuasive or expository text. It's not a debate. You don't need to argue your case and sway the reader toward your way of thinking. You don't need to interpret the meaning of your central theme or its message. You are taking your reader on a journey and telling a story. Do just that. Give them a sense of the theme and move on.

Dialogue – do or don't?

Definitely don't. This is a summary of your story, not the story itself. Tell us what we need to know and leave your sparkling banter for the pages of your manuscript.

Point of view

We've all heard time-and-time again that head-hopping in our manuscript is a no-no – that is, unless we happen to be the ever-talented Nora Roberts. With this in mind, what are the 'rules' around head-hopping in a synopsis?

Hopefully after reading Chapter 3: The structure of turning point paragraphs you'll realize that it's imperative to give the reader an understanding of both central characters' states of mind during each turning point, with an economy of words. In a synopsis, there's no time or space to do a scene-by-scene show and tell for each character. Each turning point should be dealt with clearly and concisely, but with voice and emotion. And it's important to contrast each character's emotional set at each stage in their growing relationship.

So, while head-hopping is usually a categorical no-no in your manuscript, this is not the case in your synopsis. It's perfectly acceptable to visit first your heroine, then your hero's thoughts, in successive sentences within the very same paragraph.

Rhetorical questions

As mentioned in Chapter 2: Types of hooks, it's not ideal to open or fill your synopsis with rhetorical questions. These are pet hates for many agents and editors and the last thing you want to do is alienate the person you're hoping will represent or publish your book.

If you are really fixed on including a rhetorical question, make sure you do two things:

1. Link back to the central theme and/or the central characters' GMCs.
2. Answer the question before the end of your synopsis.

Sectioning a synopsis – yes or no?

Just as your manuscript must flow, so must your synopsis. If you create sections or subheadings for different plot points or timelines, or try to introduce subplots by cordoning them off from the main part of your story, your synopsis will be jumpy and jarring and downright confusing.

Tell the story through your synopsis the same way you do in your novel, with fluidity and finesse. Don't chop it into sections and pull your reader out every time they finish one portion and enter another. Write a seamless story with no avenue for the reader to escape.

Brevity

I covered this point in Chapter 2, under the context of world-building, but I believe it merits another mention here.

There are multiple benefits to cutting superfluous words from a synopsis. Length limitation is the first that springs to mind. Depending on the target of your synopsis, submission guidelines may only allow you a couple of pages to capture the key elements of your story. Or in some cases you may have – *gulp!* – one page or less. Cutting back on unnecessary words or phrases will leave more room for content. And let's face it, the content of your story is what counts here.

Brevity increases flow and pacing. Agents and editors will look to your synopsis as a gauge of your writing acumen. A synopsis that drags can be a red flag for similar issues in a manuscript. Carve back on your words and make sure you include only major turning points and you'll demonstrate a clear understanding of not only the building blocks of a great story, but also the art and importance of pacing.

More words don't necessarily lead to more meaning. Sometimes all they do is muddy the waters so that context and content are lost in the jumble.

Vocabulary

Your choice of vocabulary impacts hugely on your synopsis. The more evocative the language, the less words you'll need to tell your story and convey emotion. With this in mind, try to incorporate strong, evocative language and cut back on unnecessary filler-type words.

To help with this, here are a few word choices and word combinations to avoid:

1. Delexical verbs

These include verbs like have, take, make, give, go and do.

These verbs shift meaning from the action verb to the noun and tend to make the sentence lengthy and awkward.

Example: *I took a shower.*

While there is nothing structurally wrong with this sentence, the alternative *'I showered'* is stronger, cleaner and more direct.

2. Phrasal verbs

These are verbs combined with a preposition that perform the same job as one verb.

Example: *He always shows up on time.*

By replacing *'shows up'* with *'arrives'* you've reduced your word count and created a more streamlined sentence.

3. Passive sentences

These are sentences where a noun is acted on by a verb and we have no idea who or what is doing this action.

Example: *The body was examined by the coroner.*

This sentence will be shorter and stronger if you make it active and tell us who did the examining: *The coroner examined the body.*

Five words instead of seven – a definite win when creating a synopsis.

4. Present perfect progressive tense

My goodness, even the name is a mouthful! PPPTs are verb tenses formed using 'has or have been' and the present participle of the verb (ending in '–ing').

Example: *Luke has been unsuccessfully trying to win an award.*

There's no hard and fast rule for rejigging this sentence into something less cumbersome. I'd suggest starting from scratch and rewording it altogether.

Luke's every effort to win an award failed.

Luke tried – continuously – to win an award. And failed.

5. Adverbs

Use adverbs sparingly, if at all. Instead of adding another word into your sentence to describe your verb, see if you can replace that verb with a stronger more evocative alternative.

Example: *Bob walked slowly toward Sandra's angry form.*

This can be rewritten as: *Bob trudged toward Sandra's angry form.*

See the difference?

In the first sentence we know Bob is walking slowly, but we have no idea why. He could be tired, have sore feet, be navigating rough terrain. Or maybe slow is just his normal walking speed.

Compare this with the second sentence where we immediately gain a sense of Bob's mood. *Collins English Dictionary* says, *'If you trudge somewhere, you walk there slowly and with heavy steps, especially because you are tired or unhappy.'* So, in this instance, we can guess that Bob is hesitant, wary, maybe even unhappy, dreading his upcoming confrontation with Sandra. And we get all this from the addition of one word.

Evocative language

The definition of 'evocative' suggests something that conjures up strong images, memories or feelings. As authors, this is – or should be – our aim when creating our story. It follows then that this should be our aim when creating our synopsis, too. At this point, I must confess my unconditional love and gratitude for my thesaurus. In those times when I need help finding the right word, this writing tool is invaluable.

When crafting your synopsis, look for descriptive words that closely convey the mood and disposition of your characters. Analyze the complexities of your character's feelings. Yes, they may be angry, but why? What caused their anger? How intense is their reaction? Are they merely annoyed or irritated? Or are they seething red-hot with rage. Every emotion has degrees. It's important to analyze the degree of emotion your character is experiencing and convey this as accurately as possible by carefully choosing your words.

The following lists are by no means exhaustive, but they should help you begin building your own store of descriptors.

Emotive verbs

Emotive verbs describe 'intense feelings'. Using an emotive verb rather than a weaker verb linked to an adverb not only cuts back on word count, but it also yields a stronger, more effective piece of writing.

Here are some examples to get you started. I've tried to group them in degrees of intensity. You may or may not agree with my categories, but just make sure you complete the analysis I outlined earlier by evaluating the intensity of your character's reaction and choose the word or words that best describe their emotional set.

EMOTIVE VERBS	
ANGER HATE	**SOFT** annoy, bother, cross, dislike, displease, foil, frustrate, irritate, peeve, rankle, thwart **MEDIUM** affront, aggravate, alienate, antagonize, bristle, dispirit, exasperate, inflame, insult, madden, offend, resent, rile, vex, wind up **STRONG** abhor, appall, avenge, despise, detest, disgust, enrage, incense, infuriate, loathe, rage, rant, rave, revolt, seethe, spite
FEAR WORRY	**SOFT** alert, brood, dread, caution, concern, confuse, contemplate, disconcert, disorient, disquiet, doubt, edgy, fidget, hesitate, jitter, ponder, shy, tense, watch **MEDIUM** agitate, alarm, distrust, fear, frighten, intimidate, perturb, rattle, scare, shake, startle, suspect, trouble, unnerve, unsettle, wary **STRONG** horrify, panic, paralyze, petrify, shock, terrify, terrorize
HAPPY CONTENT	**SOFT** amuse, calm, celebrate, encourage, hope, humor, inspire, oblige, pacify, please, smile, soothe **MEDIUM** cheer, delight, enliven, excite, fulfill, gratify, gladden, play, pride, rejuvenate, revel, satisfy **STRONG** elate, enchant, enthrall, exhilarate, jubilant, manic, radiate, rejoice, thrill
SAD UPSET	**SOFT** bemoan, complain, contemplate, disappoint, disconnect, distract, growl, grumble, hurt, move, ponder, regret, reflect, sadden **MEDIUM** afflict, deject, demoralize, discourage, disenchant, dishearten, dismay, dispirit, disillusion, drain, mourn, mull over, regret, sorrow, weep, wail, woe **STRONG** anguish, bereave, bewail, depress, despair, despond, devastate, disparage, distress, grieve, howl, lament, suffer
SHAME EMBARASS	**SOFT** abash, account, chasten, discomfit, discompose, disconcert, flush, fluster, humble, lower, perturb, put down, rattle, show up **MEDIUM** accuse, blame, criticize, denunciate, discredit, guilt, intimidate, regret, repent, reproach, rue, sully, taint, tarnish, unnerve **STRONG** adulterate, belittle, censure, condemn, corrupt, debase, defile, degrade, demean, disgrace, dishonor, distress, humiliate, impugn, impute, mortify, ostracize, reprehend, ruin, self-condemn, shame, soil, stigmatize

Active verbs

An active verb expresses something that a person, animal or object can do. By making the correct choice of verb, your word choice can also convey a sense of emotion. A character closing a door demonstrates a different emotional state to someone who slams it. And if they secure it, turn the lock and pocket the key, they are in a very different space once again.

With this list – which is only a drop in a very large ocean – I hope to further show how you can make every word in your synopsis work for you, and give your reader a better gauge of your character's emotional status.

ACTIVE VERB	POSSIBLE REPLACEMENT OPTIONS
AGREE	accept, acknowledge, allow, assent, acquiesce, concur, permit, settle, subscribe
ASK	demand, invite, needle, plead, query, question, request, solicit, summon
BREAK	bust, crack, crush, destroy, disrupt, fracture, interrupt, rest, rupture, shatter, smash, snap, tear
CALL	buzz, cry, exclaim, holler, phone, ring, scream, shout, yell
CLIMB	ascend, clamber, escalate, mount, rise, scale, scrabble, scramble, soar
CLOSE	bolt, fasten, lock, secure, seal, shut, slam
COME	appear, arrive, attain, turn up, reach, roll up
CRY	bawl, bellow, blubber, call, exclaim, holler, howl, roar, scream, shout, shriek, sob, wail, weep, yell, yelp
DIG	burrow, channel, excavate, gibe, insult, jab, jeer, mine, plow, prod, poke, taunt, tunnel
FALL	cascade, collapse, crumple, descend, drop, flop, plummet, plunge, sink, slip, stumble, trip, topple, tumble
FIND	acquire, attain, detect, discover, ferret out, locate, pinpoint, recover, regain, retrieve, realize, situate, trace, track down, uncover, unearth

GET	acquire, comprehend, develop, find, follow, gain, obtain, perceive, procure, secure, understand
GIVE	afford, allocate, allot, award, assign, bestow, dedicate, donate, grant, impart, lend, offer, provide, surrender, yield
GRAB	capture, clutch, grasp, grapple, grip, seize, snatch, steal, take
HELP	aid, amend, assist, ease, facilitate, improve, relieve, support
HIDE	conceal, cover, disappear, obscure, secrete, shroud, suppress, veil, withhold
HIT	bang, batter, beat, blow, bump, clash, cuff, knock, punch, rap, slap, smack, sock, strike, struck, thump, whack
HOLD	attach, clasp, clamp, clench, clutch, control, cuddle, embrace, enfold, fasten, grasp, grip, hug, influence, possess, power, secure, squeeze
JOIN	adhere, bind, bond, connect, fasten, fix, link, merge, paste, stick, unify, unite
JUMP	bounce, bound, flinch, hurdle, jerk, jolt, leap, lurch, spring, start, vault
LEAVE	abandon, abscond, depart, desert, disappear, ditch, drop, dump, exit, forsake, go, quit, storm off, vacate, vamoose
LIFT	boost, elevate, heave, hoist, lighten, nick, pilfer, pinch, pocket, raise, steal, take
LISTEN	attend, eavesdrop, heed, overhear, snoop
LOOK	appear, contemplate, examine, eye, focus on, gawk, gawp, gaze, glance, glare, glimpse, inspect, observe, peek, peep, peer, regard, scan, scrutinize, see, seem, stare, study, survey, view, watch
MAKE	assemble, brand, build, cause, command, compel, compose, concoct, construct, cook, craft, create, effect, fabricate, fashion, force, form, formulate, generate, order, prepare, pressure, pressurize, produce, sort, style, type, variety
MOVE	advance, budge, cause, change, dance, encourage, induce, influence, jump, nudge, prod, provoke, pull, push, realign, rearrange, redeploy, refocus, relocate, reposition, run, shift, shove, shuffle, step, stir, transfer, transport, travel, turn, walk
OPEN	accessible, agape, ajar, defenseless, expose, gaping, release, unbolt, undefended, undo, unfasten, unguarded, unhinge, unlock, unprotected, unrestricted, unseal, untie, unwrap, vulnerable

PICK	choose, elect, favor, opt, pluck, prefer, rather, select
PUSH	advocate, boost, endorse, force, goad, induce, make, persuade, plug, press, promote, ram, shove, thrust, urge
RUN	course, dart, dash, flood, flow, function, gambol, gush, hurry, jog, lope, move, operate, race, rush, sprint, scurry, stream, trickle
SAY	answer, articulate, cry, declare, disclose, exclaim, express, impart, reply, reveal, speak, state, shout, tell, utter, verbalize, voice
SPEAK	address, articulate, chat, chatter, communicate, converse, declare, lecture, preach, say, state, talk, tell, verbalize, voice
START	begin, commence, establish, flinch, initiate, jerk, jolt, jump, kick off, launch, lead, recoil, twitch
STOP	ban, bar, block, cease, discontinue, end, finish, halt, hinder, impede, intercept, obstruct, pause, prevent, rest, stay, waylay
THROW	baffle, bamboozle, bewilder, cast, chuck, confuse, disconcert, fling, flip, heave, hurl, lob, pitch, puzzle, perplex, surprise, toss
TOUCH	affect, caress, contact, converge, feel, handle, join, link, meet, move, pat, rub, stir, stroke, tap, upset
TURN	circle, pivot, revolve, rotate, spin, swivel, twirl, twist
USE	abuse, apply, consume, deplete, employ, exhaust, expend, exploit, manipulate, mistreat, spend, utilize, waste
WALK	amble, dawdle, hike, lumber, march, move, pace, plod, saunter, slog, stagger, stalk, stamp, stride, stroll, traipse, tread, trek, trudge
WANT	covet, crave, demand, desire, hanker, fancy, lack, long for, miss, need, require, wish, yearn
WASH	bath, bathe, clean, cleanse, launder, rinse, scrub, shampoo, shower, sluice, soak, sponge, swab

And there you have it – a list of dos and don'ts in relation to editing and refining your synopsis:

- » Voice
- » Tone
- » Secondary characters
- » Secondary plots
- » Explanations of central theme or message
- » Dialogue – do or don't?
- » Point of view
- » Rhetorical questions
- » Sectioning a synopsis – yes or no?
- » Brevity
- » Vocabulary
- » Evocative language

Make sure you check and apply each one of these points to your draft synopsis. Analyze your content, voice, tone and vocabulary, and ensure you've used each word, each sentence, to its utmost potential. Every word should earn its place in your writing. Every word should work to build your story, convey emotion and create atmosphere. As you craft, ensure you write mindfully and consciously to create the best synopsis you possibly can.

CHAPTER 9
THE MINI SYNOPSIS

How could I write a book on synopses without at least mentioning the mini synopsis?

In some instances, you might be required to write a shorter synopsis, something between 300 and 500 words. What should you do in this case? Exactly the same as you've done earlier, but shorter and sharper.

If you've carried out all the groundwork covered in the earlier chapters – identified your orienting information and your major turning points, created a tagline defining the central theme and high concept of your story – you'll have all the material you need. Now you must decide which of those major turning points to include and which to drop, and then piece the information together in a concise and interesting way.

Is a mini synopsis a blurb?

It is important not to confuse these two distinct constructs. Though they both have a place in the promotion of your story, they are designed for very different audiences.

A blurb is necessary for the marketing and promotion of your story from the shelves of virtual or real bookstores. It is a short outline of your story – what you'll find on the book's back cover – that often ends with a question or a hook. The goal of a blurb is to entice the reader to buy your book and read your story, and it should NOT reveal the ending. What it will do is provide a brief run-down of your characters and the central plot or theme, and it will end leaving the reader with questions. No spoilers here – the reader will need to read your story to find out what happens.

A mini synopsis is also an outline of your story, but with one very major difference: you MUST give the ending away. This is not a selling tool for the greater public; it's a tool to sell your manuscript to an agent or editor. They want the ending. They want to see that you can structure a story, and that you are able to identify the central plot or theme and provide a satisfying resolution and conclusion that readers will enjoy.

What to include in a mini synopsis?

This is a shorter, succinct version of your full synopsis. The emphasis of a mini synopsis should be around your central characters and their GMCs, with particular focus on their conflicts, i.e., what's keeping them from achieving their goals. Remember to encompass your central characters' lives at the beginning of the story, what their goals are, why they want them and what's stopping them from achieving said goals.

Deal with each central character in a separate sentence or mini-paragraph. In the case of a classic romance, one for the hero and one for the heroine.

When it comes to the turning points, *only include those that are most closely linked to the central theme of your plot*.

How many should you include? Up to three – two major turning points *and* your black moment. Unlike a standard, longer synopsis, there's no room for more.

The last part of your mini synopsis must be the resolution and conclusion. Show how the conflicts – the challenges your characters have faced – are resolved. And in the case of a romance, show the happy ever after or happy for now.

Example

Lethal in Love (Michelle Somers)

JAYDA THOMASZ was rescued when her serial killer uncle murdered her family and he was sent to prison, his serial crimes unsolved. Adopted, Jayda grows up believing a fire killed her parents and brother.

Twenty-five years later, the Night Terror killings have resurrected and Jayda's lead detective on the seemingly unsolvable investigation. A rookie moving fast up the ranks, she has much to prove. To gain intel on the latest vic, she enters a swinger's club undercover.

SETH FRIEDIN is a reporter, chasing the story that'll make his academic parents proud. When he enters the world of swinging for research, he meets an innocent whose kiss plagues his mind long after she flees.

A week later Jayda comes face-to-face with the man she's fantasized over since that kiss. Seth can't believe his luck! But moments into the seduction, Jayda gets a call – another killing. He drives her there – to the scene of her adoptive father's death.

Jayda is grief-stricken. A note implies this murder was a message, to her. She vows to catch the killer, despite being taken off the case.

Seth sees a way to get his story – get close to Jayda and help her in her quest.

Together they discover the original Night Terror is serving a life sentence for another crime. Digging deeper reveals he has a niece – her.

Devastated, Jayda finds comfort in Seth's arms, and he finds a burning need to be there for her. Together they hunt for the copycat killer – her brother, alive and well, covertly ensconced in her life as a friend.

Then she discovers Seth's secret – his news-breaking story is the story of her life.

Jayda runs to her 'friend' the moment Seth discovers he's the killer. She escapes and Seth offers her the happy ever after she never thought possible. (300 words)

Let's analyze what I have included in the synopsis above – much more than the three turning points I stipulated earlier:

1. Valuable backstory that underpins the central conflicts of the story, particularly Jayda's.
2. Orientation encompassing both Jayda's and Seth's goals, motivations and conflicts.
3. Major turning points, including the 'inciting incident' meet cute and first kiss, and the 'opportunity knocks' where Seth works with Jayda to find the killer and get his story.
4. The 'higher stakes' turning point for Jayda where the case becomes more than just a job – it becomes personal.
5. The 'making progress' turning point where they discover the Night Terror's identity and Jayda turns to Seth for comfort and support.
6. The 'no turning back' turning point where Jayda and Seth discover they want to be there for each other – a pivotal turning point in terms of their relationship as well as the plot.
7. The black moment – both romantic and plot-based.
8. The resolution and conclusion – a happy ever after.

All this, in 300 words. And if I had 500, imagine how much more I could include.

Here's another example. This synopsis was part of an entry into Romance Writers of Australia's Ripping Start Competition. In three instances, three judges gave the author full points. When you read on, you'll see why.

The Dating Deal (unpublished manuscript by Miranda Morgan)

Still reeling from her finance's death five years ago, BETH HARMONY wants only to be left alone with her quiet career as a research scientist. But as maid of honor in her cousin's impending wedding, and with her family's persistent matchmaking, Beth invents an emergency boyfriend.

Pro footballer DAN MYERS knows two things: football and 'a good time'. Two years ago he was passed over for the team captaincy, and he's not about to let his reputation off-field get in the way again.

When Beth asks the sexy stranger she's trapped in a lift with to masquerade as her boyfriend, the encounter ends in a kiss. Soon she discovers he's her cousin's best man and that images of their heart-racing embrace have gone viral.

For a woman who's never felt like she fits in, the resulting media furor causes her to retreat, but Dan's determined to continue the relationship farce or he can kiss the captaincy goodbye. With his easy confidence he helps her through her anxiety, but being around a woman of superior intellect sets off his own feelings of inadequacy surrounding the dyslexia he's kept secret for years.

It may be a relationship of convenience, but forced together they find an undeniable sexual attraction. What was meant to banish each other out of their systems does the complete opposite.

When the paparazzi become aggressive and Beth's house is broken into, Dan realizes he must leave in order to keep her safe.

Heartbroken, Beth is determined to change his mind. Enlisting help, she undergoes a makeover and confronts Dan at a benefit dinner. She publicly declares her feelings, drawing on what he taught her, and asks him to declare his dyslexia, removing its power.

> *Openly affectionate, Beth and Dan dance at the wedding, ready to face the world together.* (300 words)

In 300 words, Miranda has provided a clear picture of her central characters Beth and Dan, their GMCs, the major turning points in their relationship and the black moment – all pivotal events leading to the resolution and conclusion, a life where Dan is open about his dyslexia and the couple are ready to publicly display their relationship to the rest of the world.

This cleverly crafted piece of writing well deserves its placing in the Ripping Start contest. It does everything a mini synopsis should do, and it does it succinctly, interestingly and in Miranda's unique voice.

Your turn . . .

It's time to craft your own mini synopsis. Consider your current work in progress, or a story you've written in the past, and extract the key elements for your mini synopsis by completing the following table:

MINI SYNOPSIS BREAKDOWN

GMC Character 1:

GMC Character 2:

TURNING POINT 1:

TURNING POINT 2:

BLACK MOMENT:

RESOLUTION:

CONCLUSION:

Now, assemble all the individual parts together, to form your mini synopsis:

MINI SYNOPSIS CONSTRUCTION

The 100-word mini-mini synopsis

So, we started with two pages and now you want us to cut that back to 100 words? Are you nuts?

I hear you! It seems an impossible task. Then again, before you read this book, a synopsis seemed an impossible task and look where you are now. So, let's see how we go about crafting the 100-word synopsis.

Where do we start? Much the same as for the 300-word synopsis, but we need to go briefer again. As with any synopsis, you must introduce your central characters. This should be done in two sentences, one for each character.

Next comes the guts of your synopsis – the key challenge or premise of your book. This will be easy if you've already crafted a longer synopsis, as you will have identified the premise, perhaps even written a logline, as part of your orienting paragraphs.

Then you have one more sentence to craft – the resolution. What must your central characters do to resolve the central conflict in the story?

And that's it! Four sentences, 100 words and you have your synopsis. Simple, right? Perhaps not yet, so let's further simplify the process.

100-word mini-mini synopsis structure

There are four key parts to your 100-word synopsis:

1. Introduce the first central character, outlining their goal, motivation and conflict.
2. Introduce the second central character, outlining their goal, motivation and conflict.
3. Outline the major turning point that is linked closest to the central theme/conflict of your story.
4. Show resolution of this central conflict and the conclusive happy ever after or happy for now.

Now let's look at some examples of how to put these building blocks to use:

Lethal in Love (Michelle Somers)

I've tried to make this spoiler-free, but hopefully you'll get the idea.

> *Homicide detective JAYDA THOMASZ wants safety for the women of Melbourne. So when a serial killer reemerges after 25 years, she'll do anything to catch him. Even team up with an insufferable, sexy reporter.*

> *SETH FRIEDIN is chasing the story that'll fast-track his career, and Jayda can help – if only she wasn't so damned stubborn.*

> *Then the Night Terror moves in, threatening family, security – everything Jayda holds dear. Seth is the only one she can trust. When she falls prey to the killer's web, Seth deciphers the clues and finds her, disabling the killer, saving the woman he loves.*

Storm Clouds (Bronwyn Parry)

> *National Parks ranger ERIN TAYLOR loves her job, is falling for her colleague, SIMON KENNEDY, and is finally leaving her past behind.*

> *Until a woman is murdered: Simon's wife, who he's not seen in fourteen years. On the edge of the wilderness, an alternative lifestyle community denies knowing the deceased, but Simon and Erin suspect otherwise.*

> *As Simon uncovers a web of lies, decades old, Erin infiltrates the group and finds a charismatic, manipulative cult leader striving for ultimate control of his followers. Isolated by wild weather, Erin and Simon must race to expose the truth and prevent a tragedy.*

Dead Heat (Bronwyn Parry)

National Parks Ranger JO LOCKWOOD is often alone in the wilderness, and she likes it that way – until she discovers the body of a man, brutally murdered. Detective NICK MATHESON knows organized crime from the inside out, and suspects that the victim in the park is not an isolated murder.

Jo has seen a killer's face, and now she's at risk. Nick's determined to protect her, but as the body count starts mounting, his past and present collide. Trapped in rugged country in scorching summer heat, Nick and Jo will need to trust each other completely in order to survive.

Cinderella

CINDERELLA wants more than a life of rags and her step-mother's wrath. She wants the love and respect she shared with her father – only he's dead and now she's a slave in her own home.

PRINCE CHARMING wants a wife who's pretty and clever – like the girl he fell in love with at the royal ball. Only she vanished, her glass slipper the only proof she wasn't a dream.

As he searches for his true love, house-by-house, an imprisoned Cinderella must escape her stepmother's clutches in time to prove she's the true owner of the slipper and the prince's heart.

The perfect happy ever after.

Each of these examples is quite unique, yet notice how they all introduce the central characters, their central goal and conflict, the black moment, and then the resulting resolution and conclusion. These details are the bones of the mini-mini synopsis. How you deliver them is up to you.

Your turn . . .

This is your opportunity to practice the skills you've just learned. Why not take your mini synopsis from the section above and reduce it further to form a 100-word mini-mini synopsis?

Next, think of one or two of your favorite movies, identify the central characters' GMCs and the turning point linked closest to the premise, then formulate a mini-mini synopsis, adding in your final concluding sentence. Use the following tables to help you.

MINI-MINI SYNOPSIS BREAKDOWN

GMC Character 1:

GMC Character 2:

TURNING POINT LINKED TO PREMISE:

RESOLUTION/CONCLUSION:

MINI-MINI SYNOPSIS CONSTRUCTION

How did you go?

Now you have the structure and one or more mini-mini synopses under your belt, you're ready for the final step toward perfecting your synopsis.

CHAPTER 10
FORMATTING YOUR SYNOPSIS

If you are preparing a synopsis as part of a competition or manuscript submission, make sure you check the relevant website or blog for submission guidelines. For manuscript submissions, each agent or editor will have their own formatting preferences and it is important you carefully follow their instructions. When it comes to the synopsis, some might want single spacing; others might want double. Some might request that the text be pasted into the body of the email; others might want it as an attachment.

If you're preparing multiple submissions, make sure you cater for each set of submission guidelines. It may mean saving different versions of your synopsis, perhaps one long, one medium length and one short. It may also mean you need to format each individually, depending on guideline preferences.

And I can't stress this enough – make sure you provide only what's been requested. More isn't necessarily more, in this case. If no page length is specified, don't send more than a three-page synopsis. If the request is for a 'brief synopsis', make sure it's brief – no more than one page, less if you can manage it.

If no guidelines are available, here's a fallback list of formatting guidelines to help you out:

» **Spacing:** for a one-page synopsis, use single spacing with a space in between paragraphs. For two or more pages, use double-spacing.

- » **Alignment:** left alignment with no paragraph indentations for a single-spaced synopsis. Left alignment with half-inch indentation for a double-spaced synopsis.
- » **Margins:** one-inch margins all around.
- » **Font:** type in a plain font, usually 12 point Times New Roman.
- » **Headers:** 'author's name/book title' on the left (Michelle Somers/*Lethal in Love*) and page numbers on the right.
- » **Point of view:** always write a synopsis in an active voice, third person, present tense *regardless of the tense and point of view of your novel*.
- » **Central characters:** the first mention of protagonist(s) – the hero and heroine in the case of a classic romance – should include both first name and surname in uppercase.

While the outline above is the nuts and bolts of synopsis formatting, don't forget the organization of your content using the *Simply Synopsis* structure:

1. Orientation
2. Major turning points
3. Resolution
4. Conclusion

And with the above in mind, you're ready to send off your synopsis.

Good luck!

CHAPTER 11
SYNOPSIS EXAMPLE

What's a 'how to' book without examples?

I thought it would be useful to work through one example together, beginning to end. For this purpose I've chosen one of my all-time favorite Disney movies, *Aladdin*.

Let's take a closer look at the process we'll follow before we begin:

1. Identify the major turning points of the story.
2. Categorize each major turning point as either a plot point, character arc or romance arc.
3. Group these turning points into paragraphs to form the body of the synopsis.
4. Formulate the central characters' GMCs.
5. Create the orientation paragraphs incorporating hook, world-building, central theme and central characters.
6. Consider any backstory that gives context to the central characters GMCs.
7. Put it all together, edit and format, *et voilá*! you've built your synopsis!

If you've read each chapter and worked through the exercises, this will be a consolidation of what you already know.

So, let's begin . . .

Disney's *Aladdin*

Turning points and major plot events

For the purpose of this exercise, I analyzed the story and pulled out all the plot points I felt were important. I identified twenty.

1. Royal vizier Jafar uses a scarab beetle to open the Cave of Wonders and sends a man in after the magic lamp he desires. The cave entrance swallows the man, declaring only 'the diamond in the rough' can enter.

2. A royal prince calls Aladdin a 'worthless street rat' and Aladdin vows to Abu the monkey that one day things will get better.

3. Next day, that same royal prince storms out of the palace after Princess Jasmine's pet tiger, Rajah, chases him away.

4. Later that day, Jasmine slips out of the palace in disguise. In a street market she gives an apple to a hungry boy and the street merchant threatens to chop off her hand unless she can pay for it. Aladdin intervenes and whisks Jasmine away.

5. Jafar uses the sultan's blue diamond ring with the Sands of Time, identifying 'the diamond in the rough' as Aladdin.

6. Aladdin and Abu take Jasmine to their hideaway. Aladdin and Jasmine share how they both feel trapped in their lives. The royal guards arrive and grab Aladdin. Jasmine reveals herself and demands they set him free. They refuse. They only take orders from Jafar.

7. Jasmine confronts Jafar. He falsely informs her Aladdin has been executed for kidnapping the princess. Jasmine runs away in tears.

8. Aladdin is imprisoned in the royal dungeon where he meets Jafar disguised as an old prisoner. Jafar claims he needs Aladdin's help to locate the Cave of Wonders and promises Aladdin riches to win the love of any princess.

9. Abu helps them escape. Aladdin enters the Cave of Wonders, with strict instructions to 'touch nothing but the lamp'. Aladdin finds the lamp but Abu touches a large ruby, causing the cave to collapse. They make it to the entrance and Jafar takes the lamp, then tries to kill Aladdin. Abu bites Jafar and rescues the lamp, and he and Aladdin fall back into the cavern.

10. Aladdin examines the lamp, rubs it and a genie appears. He gets three wishes. He tricks the genie into getting him out of the cave on a magic carpet without using a wish. As he considers his wishes, Genie reveals he'd wish to be free of the lamp. Aladdin promises to free him with his third wish. His first wish is to be a prince so he can win Princess Jasmine.

11. Without the lamp, Jafar must gain power by different means. He attempts to convince the Sultan to let him marry Jasmine.

12. Prince Ali Ababwa (aka Aladdin) enters the Kingdom in a procession – the Sultan is impressed, Jafar is suspicious and Jasmine is less-than-interested. Prince Ali visits Jasmine on her balcony and she rebuffs his charms. He steps over the edge and onto the magic carpet. Jasmine is intrigued, plus something about Ali reminds her of the street urchin she liked. They journey round the world on the carpet and share a kiss. Aladdin admits he's the urchin Jasmin met, but his real identity is Prince Ali. He tells Jasmine he likes to escape the palace and its restraints, just like her.

13. After Aladdin leaves Jasmine, palace guards tie him up and dump him in a nearby lake. He uses his second wish to save his life. Aladdin returns to the palace to find Jafar using his cobra-shaped staff to hypnotize the sultan into letting him marry Jasmine. Aladdin smashes the staff and Jafar vanishes.

14. The sultan sees that Jasmine loves Aladdin and gives his blessing for their marriage.

15. Jasmine tells Aladdin that after they marry he'll become sultan and rule Agrabah. Aladdin is shocked. He can't rule Agrabah.

On top of that, he hates that he's not a real prince and has to continue lying to the princess. Genie tries to convince him to tell Jasmine the truth and use his third wish to free him. Aladdin can't do it. He won't lose everything he's gained. The genie retreats into the lamp, feeling betrayed.

16. Jafar steals the lamp and summons the genie. He wishes to become a powerful sorcerer and reveals Aladdin's true identity to the princess before banishing him to a wintry mountain region. Jafar uses his second wish to become sultan, imprisoning the princess until she agrees to marry him.

17. Aladdin finds the magic carpet and returns to the palace, determined to right his wrongs. He sneaks in to steal back the lamp while Jasmine distracts Jafar, but Jafar sees him, shoving him away, trapping Jasmine in a large hourglass. Jafar transforms into a giant cobra and the two engage in a battle – to the death.

18. The sands in the hourglass rise and time is running out. Aladdin taunts Jafar for not being the most powerful being. He'll never be as great as the genie. Jafar wishes to be a genie and Genie complies. Jafar is jubilant, until he is shackled and sucked into the new lamp created by his wish.

19. Genie hurls Jafar's lamp into the Cave of Wonders and offers to make Aladdin a prince again with his third and final wish. Aladdin is done. No longer will he pretend to be something he's not. He makes his third wish. Genie's shackles fall away. He is free! The sultan proclaims a new law allowing Aladdin to marry Jasmine even though he's not a prince.

20. Aladdin and the princess marry and Aladdin becomes heir to the kingdom. They fly away into the big blue yonder on the magic carpet.

And there it is. Twenty plot points that comprise the story of Disney's *Aladdin*.

Now we have our summary, we must decide what plot points to include in the synopsis and what to leave out. This decision will largely depend on the genre. Because this book's main focus is romance, our synopsis will need a romantic perspective. Therefore, we must choose plot points that directly impact on Aladdin and Jasmine's developing relationship.

For genres other than romance, it's important to focus on the plot points that impact both story and character arc. In some instances, as is the case with *Aladdin*, these plot points will be closely linked to the romance. This means your choice of plot points will be much the same in both instances, and the main difference will lie in perspective and delivery of these points within the body of your synopsis.

If romance is our key focus here, can you pick which of *Aladdin's* plot points pass the test? Once you've chosen, keep reading and see whether your choices match mine.

Turning-point analysis

Let's catalogue our twenty turning points into three categories: plot points, character arc and romance arc. As we do this, it's important to begin teasing out the emotions and state of mind for each central character at each crucial stage. Start incorporating the six key elements from Chapter 3: Six-step structure for major turning points. The more information you include here, the easier it will be when you start writing your synopsis.

	PLOT POINT	CHARACTER ARC	ROMANCE ARC
1	Jafar opens the Cave of Wonders and sends a man in. The cave swallows the man, declaring only 'the diamond in the rough' can enter.		
2	A royal prince calls Aladdin a 'worthless street rat'.	GMC (MOTIVATION) Aladdin vows that one day things will get better.	
3	The royal prince storms out of the palace after Princess Jasmine fends off his advances.	GMC (GOAL) Jasmine does not want to marry someone she doesn't love, and she won't be bought.	

		GMC (CONFLICT)	INCITING INCIDENT / MEET CUTE
4	Jasmine leaves the palace disguised. She gives an apple to a hungry boy and is threatened by the street merchant.	She craves freedom, the chance to be who she wants and to do what she wants. But she can't, because she's a princess and must follow Agraban law.	Aladdin saves Jasmine and whisks her away to his hideout.
5	Jafar consults the Sands of Time discovering 'the diamond in the rough' is Aladdin.		
6	Jasmine and Aladdin talk. Royal guards arrive and grab Aladdin. Jasmine reveals herself and demands they free him. They refuse.	As they talk, they both feel accepted for themselves not the labels society places on them. Jasmine reveals her identity to the guards to save Aladdin, disregarding the consequences of leaving the palace.	**FIRST CONNECTION** They share how trapped they both feel in their lives.
7	Jafar lies about Aladdin's fate. Jasmine runs away in tears.	Jasmine blames herself for Aladdin's fate and feels even more 'trapped' than ever, after experiencing what true connection feels like.	
8	**OPPORTUNITY KNOCKS** In the royal dungeon, Aladdin meets Jafar disguised as an old prisoner. He tempts Aladdin with promises of riches from The Cave of Wonders.	**GMC (CONFLICT)** Aladdin believes he needs these riches to win the love of the princess, that he's not good enough without them.	
9	They escape. Aladdin enters the cave and finds the lamp. The cave collapses but he makes it to the entrance, passing the lamp to Jafar just as the vizier pulls out a knife. Aladdin and lamp fall back into the cavern.	Aladdin risks his life and enters the cave, all to get the riches to win the princess. This shows his lack of self-worth, his belief that he needs wealth to win love and acceptance.	
10	**FORK IN THE ROAD** Aladdin rubs the lamp and a genie appears. He gets three wishes. He tricks Genie into getting him out of the cave on a magic carpet without using a wish.	Aladdin shows a careless regard for the genie's powers, acting as if the whole situation is just a bit of fun. This is a precursor to his carelessness later that allows Jafar to steal the lamp.	
11	Without the lamp, Jafar attempts to convince the sultan to let him marry Jasmine so he can gain the power he craves.		
12	**PROGRESS** Prince Ali Ababwa arrives in Agrabah. His wealth impresses the sultan. Not so Jasmine. Later, he visits her balcony and they journey round the world on the carpet.	**GMC (MOTIVATION)** Pomp and ceremony do not impress Jasmine. They represent another stuck up, self-absorbed prince interested in her father's kingdom, not her. **GMC (GOAL)** She is searching for something genuine. Something real and true, like she shared with the urchin she met, then lost.	Jasmine rebuffs Ali, then sees something of the urchin in him. She trusts him enough to join him on a magic carpet ride. Aladdin admits he's the urchin she met but he adopts the disguise to escape palace life. . . . and his spiral of lies begins. Jasmine feels that **CONNECTION** again. Ali gets her. They share their **FIRST KISS**.
13	After Aladdin leaves Jasmine, palace guards bind him and dump him in a nearby lake. He rubs the lamp and uses his second wish to save his life. Aladdin returns to the palace to find Jafar using his staff to hypnotize the sultan into letting him marry Jasmine. Aladdin smashes the staff and Jafar vanishes.		Aladdin saves the sultan from hypnosis and Jasmine from marrying Jafar. He is winning her respect and admiration. Jasmine once again sees Aladdin as her savior.

#			
14	The sultan is delighted to discover that Jasmine loves Aladdin and gives his blessing for marriage.	**GOALS ACHIEVED** Jasmine can marry for love and Aladdin gets the princess.	**GOALS ACHIEVED NO TURNING BACK NOW** On the surface it seems that the couple have won their HEA. They admit their love and commit to each other.
15	**HEART'S TALK** Jasmine and Aladdin talk. Jasmine reveals Aladdin will become sultan and rule Agrabah after they marry. Genie suggests Aladdin tell the truth and free him. **MOMENT OF TRUTH** Aladdin won't do it – he won't risk losing Jasmine. An angry genie retreats into the lamp. Aladdin tosses the lamp and storms off.	Aladdin is stunned. He hadn't thought past winning Jasmine's love. He's not ready to be sultan and rule a country. **GMC (CONFLICT)** Aladdin feels the weight of his lies. He hates that he's not a real prince and has to keep lying to the princess. He's angry he let the genie down, but feels trapped. He can't free him without losing the princess.	**FALSE GOAL** Aladdin realizes the riches aren't what he really wanted – he wants Jasmine. But without having to pretend to be something he's not. His lies make him feel anger toward himself and uncomfortable with Jasmine, but he sees no clear way out of the situation.
16	**BLACK MOMENT** Jafar steals the lamp and summons the genie, wishing to become a powerful sorcerer. He reveals Aladdin's true identity and banishes him, using his second wish to become sultan, imprisoning the princess until she agrees to marry him.	**MOMENT OF TRUTH** Aladdin realizes his choices led to this – the lies, breaking his promise to the genie, pretending to be someone he's not. His guilt is overwhelming. He must return to Agrabah as Aladdin and set things right.	**BLACK MOMENT / ALL IS LOST** Jasmine believes everything about Aladdin was a lie, including his feelings for her. Aladdin believes he has endangered the princess and lost her love and respect. And his actions put the city of Agrabah and its people at risk.
17	**CLIMAX** Aladdin returns to the palace. He tries to steal back the lamp, but Jafar sees him and knocks him away, trapping Jasmine in a large hourglass. Jafar transforms into a giant cobra and a fight ensues.	**CHARACTER GROWTH** Aladdin fights to save Jasmine, despite knowing he'll never be a prince and therefore can never marry her.	**CLIMAX** Aladdin and Jasmine work together to fight Jafar and win back the kingdom. To do this, they must trust each other once again.
18	Jasmine is almost buried by the hourglass sand. In a panic, Aladdin tells Jafar he'll never be as powerful as Genie. Enraged, Jafar makes the wish and Genie complies. Jafar is jubilant, until he's shackled and sucked into his lamp. Genie hurls Jafar into the Cave of Wonders.	Aladdin owns up to his lies and apologizes to Jasmine.	Aladdin and Jasmine rejoice in being free. Jasmine accepts Aladdin's apology and forgives him, but despairs over not being able to choose him as a suitor. He has won back her trust and her love.
19	**RESOLUTION** Genie offers to make Aladdin a prince again with his third and final wish. Aladdin makes a wish. Genie's shackles fall away. He is free! The sultan announces Aladdin has demonstrated his worth and proclaims a new law – Aladdin can marry the princess.	**CHARACTER GROWTH** Aladdin is done. He'll no longer pretend to be something he's not. He frees the genie knowing he can't be a prince without him.	**RESOLUTION** Aladdin can marry Jasmine even though he's not a prince.
20	**CONCLUSION** Aladdin and Jasmine are married and Aladdin becomes heir to the kingdom.		**CONCLUSION** Aladdin and Jasmine fly away into the big blue yonder on the magic carpet. **HAPPY EVER AFTER**

Great job! We've analyzed the story and identified the plot points leading to either character or romance development. Now we can start forming our synopsis.

Our final major turning points

This is a synopsis for romance so we must shave away all unnecessary plot points and secondary characters until we are left with Aladdin and Jasmine's story. I managed to condense the story into nine major turning points. Depending on the required length of your synopsis, you can expand or contract on these nine key points.

INCITING INCIDENT = MEET CUTE

Jasmine rebuffs a suitor and escapes the palace disguised.
She gives an apple to a hungry boy and is threatened by the street merchant.
Aladdin whisks her away to his hideaway.

▼

CONNECTION

Jasmine and Aladdin share how they feel trapped.
Royal guards arrive and grab Aladdin. Jasmine reveals herself and demands they free him. They refuse.
Jafar lies about Aladdin's fate. Jasmine runs away in tears.

▼

OPPORTUNITY KNOCKS / FORK IN THE ROAD

Jafar tricks Aladdin into escaping the royal dungeon and entering The Cave of Wonders.
Aladdin finds the lamp but gets trapped inside the cave. He rubs the lamp and a genie offers him three wishes.
He tricks Genie into freeing him without using a wish.

▼

MAKING (FALSE) PROGRESS = DECEPTION

Prince Ali Ababwa arrives in Agrabah. He impresses the Sultan. Not Jasmine.
Later, he visits Jasmine's balcony and she sees something of the boy who saved her in him.
They journey round the world on the magic carpet and Ali reveals he's the urchin she met earlier.
They talk and share their FIRST KISS. They connect, but this connection is based on lies.

▼

NO TURNING BACK NOW

Aladdin leaves Jasmine only to be captured by palace guards and dumped in a nearby lake.
He uses his second wish to save his life and returns to the palace to find Jafar hypnotizing the sultan into
letting him marry Jasmine. Aladdin smashes the hypnotic staff and Jafar vanishes.
The sultan sees that Jasmine loves Aladdin and gives his blessing for marriage.

▼

HIGHER STAKES / MOMENT OF TRUTH

Jasmine reveals that Aladdin will become sultan and rule Agrabah when they marry.
Aladdin is stunned and hit with feelings of inadequacy. Genie suggests Aladdin tell the truth and free him.
Aladdin refuses. An angry Genie retreats into the lamp. Aladdin tosses the lamp and storms off.

▼

BLACK MOMENT (ALL IS LOST)

Jafar steals the lamp and wishes to become a powerful sorcerer.
He reveals Aladdin's true identity and banishes him, using his second wish to become sultan, imprisoning the
princess until she agrees to marry him.

▼

RESOLUTION

Aladdin returns and fights Jafar, taunting he'll never be as powerful as Genie. Jafar makes the wish, becomes a
genie and is shackled and sucked into his lamp. Genie hurls Jafar into the Cave of Wonders.
Genie offers to make Aladdin a prince again with his third and final wish. Aladdin won't lie anymore - he
wishes for Genie's freedom.
The sultan proclaims a new law, and Aladdin can marry Jasmine.

▼

CONCLUSION = HAPPY EVER AFTER

Aladdin and Jasmine fly away on the magic carpet.

Central character GMC

Now we have our turning points, let's break this down and analyze
Aladdin and Jasmine's central goals, motivations and conflicts.

Aladdin

What's Aladdin's dream/goal?

From the moment we meet Aladdin, we are thrust deep into his point
of view and clearly see his external goal is to have a better life. We
see him gazing out toward the palace, imagining what it would be
like to live there. Then he meets Princess Jasmine and his dream
expands – he wants to marry her.

His internal goal is a little tougher to find, but if we dig deeper,
we realize he wants to feel valued. Accepted. Appreciated. Loved.

Why does he want these things?

Aladdin's motivation is straightforward: he's a street urchin with
nothing but the clothes on his back. He has no family, no friends
but his monkey companion, Abu, no one to call his own. Quite simply,
he wants the reverse of his situation – to belong, to have a home
and people around him who care.

What's standing between him and his external goal?
Well, there's the obvious 'he's a street urchin and has no money or means' reason. I'm sure in Agrabah it's highly unlikely for someone like Aladdin to transcend classes. And I imagine the laws of the land, as well as its people – the royal prince, for one – keep him firmly fixed in his place.

How does this link with his internal goal?
Not only must Aladdin fight internal feelings of worthlessness, but he's surrounded by people who see him in the same light – the royal prince and the royal guards are two obvious examples.

Princess Jasmine

What's Jasmine's dream/goal?
Jasmine's character is less complex than Aladdin's. She wants to marry for love, to choose her husband and not have him chosen for her. She wants to feel 'normal', to have control over her life rather than being controlled. And more, she wants to be loved for who she is, not whose daughter she is.

And her internal goal? She wants to stop feeling powerless, to stop feeling trapped in her life and the palace walls.

Why does she want these things?
Here we have a princess stuck in a world where her decisions aren't her own. She's governed by Agraban law which states that she must marry a prince. Problem is, all the princes she's met are pompous, arrogant and only interested in her for the associated position of sultan.

What's standing between her and her goals?
Well, just the small matter of Agraban law – only a prince can marry a princess. Plus, she loves and respects her father too much to blatantly go against his wishes.

Now let's summarize both characters' GMCs in a table:

Name: ALADDIN
Occupation: Street urchin

	EXTERNAL	INTERNAL
G O A L	**WANTS** to have a better life. **WANTS** to live in the palace and marry the princess.	**WANTS** to feel valued, accepted, appreciated and loved.
M O T I V A T I O N	**BECAUSE** he's sick of being a street urchin with no home, no food, nothing to call his own.	**BECAUSE** he wants people see him as more than a street urchin and for them to value the person he is behind the scruffy, poor exterior.
C O N F L I C T	**BUT** he has no money and no means to change this.	**BUT** he's been viewed as worthless and insignificant for so long, that's how he feels inside.

Name: JASMINE
Occupation: Princess

	EXTERNAL	INTERNAL
G O A L	**WANTS** to choose her husband, not have him chosen for her.	**WANTS** to be loved for who she is, not whose daughter she is. **WANTS** to stop feeling trapped and powerless.
M O T I V A T I O N	**BECAUSE** she wants to marry for love.	**BECAUSE** she wants happiness and love. **BECAUSE** she wants control over her own destiny.
C O N F L I C T	**BUT** Agraban law states she must marry a prince. **BUT** all the princes she's met are pompous, arrogant and only interested in her for the associated position of sultan.	**BUT** she's governed by her father, the sultan, and Agraban law, and she has no power to choose what she wants.

Phew! That's the hard work done. Now all that's left is to write our synopsis. Let's look at a series of examples of differing lengths.

Disney's *Aladdin* synopsis examples
Tagline

> 1. *A title does not a prince make.*
>
> 2. *Seek beyond the surface for the diamond in the rough.*
>
> 3. *First impressions are not always true.*
>
> 4. *Substance stems from your soul not the clothes on your back.*

Mini-mini synopsis (100 words)

> *ALADDIN wants a family, a home and the heart of a princess – pipedreams for an unlovable street urchin like him.*
>
> *PRINCESS JASMINE wants to meet a man she likes and to marry for love, if only Agraban law didn't require a princess to marry a prince.*
>
> *Just as Aladdin despairs of realizing his dream, he finds a magic lamp, a genie and three wishes. He transforms into a prince, winning the princess's love. When the sultan's vizier steals the lamp and captures the kingdom, Aladdin must own up to his lies, fight his self-doubts and save the woman he loves.*

Mini synopsis (300 words)

> *Street urchin ALADDIN wants the family he never had, the security of a home and to win the heart of a princess. If only he weren't poor, penniless and as far from a prince as a boy can be.*
>
> *PRINCESS JASMINE is sick of stuffy suitors who want her for her father's kingdom. She wants to meet a man she likes and to marry for love, if only Agraban law didn't forbid a princess to marry anyone but a prince.*

Disguised, Jasmine escapes the palace and finds trouble in the market, only to be whisked to safety by Aladdin. They share feelings of being trapped, but Aladdin is arrested by the royal guards before they can share more. He discovers Jasmine is a princess.

Royal vizier, Jafar, tells a heartbroken Jasmine that Aladdin was executed for kidnapping her.

Aladdin despairs of winning the princess's love. Then he finds a magic lamp and genie to transform him into a prince. As Prince Ali he woos Jasmine, believing the image makes him more worthy. Much as his lies niggle his conscience, he won't reveal the truth and free the genie from his lamp. Not if it means losing Jasmine.

Jafar steals the lamp and becomes an all-powerful sorcerer. He exposes Aladdin and banishes him from the city, seizing Agrabah, imprisoning a devastated Jasmine until she agrees to marry him.

A determined Aladdin returns to Agrabah to set his wrongs to right, knowing he can never marry Jasmine. He fights bravely, yet all seems lost until he tricks Jafar into wishing he were a genie. The vizier is sucked into his lamp and Agrabah is saved. The sultan declares Aladdin worthy of marrying his daughter.

Overjoyed, the couple fly away on a magic carpet to begin their new lives as prince and princess.

Medium synopsis (600 words/2 pages double-spaced)

In Agrabah, only a prince can marry a princess.

Street urchin ALADDIN wants the family he never had, the security of a home and to win the heart of a princess. If only he weren't poor, penniless and as far from a prince as a boy can be.

PRINCESS JASMINE is sick of stuffy suitors who want her for her father's kingdom. She wants to marry a man she loves, if only it wasn't for that little matter of a law.

Outside the palace, a royal prince calls Aladdin a 'worthless street rat'. Indignant, Aladdin vows someday to be more.

Disguised as a commoner, Jasmine escapes the suffocation of the palace. Venturing into the market, she encounters trouble, only to be whisked to safety by Aladdin. Jasmine is charmed, Aladdin is enchanted. They share feelings of being trapped, but before they can share more Aladdin is arrested by the royal guards. Jasmine reveals herself, demanding they free him. They refuse, telling her to take it up with royal vizier, Jafar.

Jafar informs a heartbroken Jasmine the urchin was executed.

Aladdin is very much alive after Jafar recognized him as 'the diamond in the rough' – the one person who can safely enter the Cave of Wonders to retrieve the magic lamp he desires.

In the royal dungeon, Aladdin despairs over winning the princess's love. Jafar appears in disguise, offering to lead him to riches enough to win any princess's heart.

Filled with new hope, Aladdin escapes and journeys to the Cave of Wonders. He finds the lamp, but the cave collapses before he hands it to Jafar. Trapped, he rubs the metal, releasing a genie who frees him from the cave on a magic carpet.

Genie offers him three wishes, divulging his desire to be freed from the lamp. With a promise to use his third wish to do this, Aladdin wishes to be a prince. Finally, his dreams are reality. He's not worthless or a street rat. He's someone who matters – Prince Ali.

Jasmine is unimpressed with Prince Ali's pomp and ceremony, until he appears on a magic carpet, asking her to trust him as did the boy who saved her. They journey around the world and Aladdin 'admits' he dresses as an urchin to escape the suffocation of palace life. Jasmine is captivated – finally someone who 'gets' how she feels! They kiss.

Head in the clouds, Aladdin leaves and is seized by Jafar's guards, forcing him to use his second wish to escape. Returning to the palace, he interrupts Jafar hypnotizing the sultan. Jafar vanishes and Jasmine rushes into Aladdin's arms. Delighted, the sultan gives them his blessing. An ecstatic Jasmine declares Aladdin will be sultan once they are married.

Consumed by feelings of worthlessness, Aladdin is torn. But much as his deception niggles, he won't reveal the truth and free the genie. Not if it means losing Jasmine.

Then Jafar steals the lamp. Now an all-powerful sorcerer, he exposes Aladdin and banishes him from the city, seizing Agrabah, imprisoning a disillusioned Jasmine until she agrees to marry him.

Aladdin returns to Agrabah, determined to right his wrongs, knowing he can never marry Jasmine. He fights bravely, yet all seems lost until he tricks Jafar into becoming a genie. Jafar is sucked into his lamp and Agrabah is saved. Aladdin refuses Genie's offer to make him a prince, freeing him instead – he won't pretend any longer.

Impressed, the sultan declares a new law: his daughter can choose any suitor. Jasmine chooses Aladdin.

Overjoyed, the couple fly away on the magic carpet, launching their new life as prince and princess.

Long synopsis (1,136 words/4 pages double-spaced)

In the Arabian town of Agrabah, only a prince can marry a princess.

Street urchin ALADDIN wants the family he never had, the security of a home and to win the heart of a princess. If only he weren't poor, penniless and as far from a prince as a boy can be.

PRINCESS JASMINE is sick of stuffy suitors who want to marry her for her father's kingdom. She wants to marry for love, if only it wasn't for that little matter of Agraban law.

After sending yet another prince packing, Princess Jasmine escapes the suffocation of the palace for a taste of freedom. Disguised as a commoner, she wanders through a market feeling relaxed and relieved, like any other ordinary girl. She spies a hungry child and offers him an apple from a stall. The merchant grabs her hand and threatens to cut it off if she doesn't pay.

Aladdin spots a beautiful girl in trouble and whisks her away to the safety of his hideout. They share a moment, an apple and a heart-to-heart conversation. Overlooking the palace, Aladdin sees his dream life; Jasmine sees the chains she longs to escape. But they both share one thing – the feeling of being trapped. Aladdin is nothing like Jasmine's suitors and everything she's looking for. He's cute, funny and kind, and he sees her as a person not a princess. Their gazes lock and they lean in.

Royal guards storm the hideout and arrest Aladdin before they can do more. Outraged, Jasmine reveals herself and orders the guards to set Aladdin free. They refuse. She must take the matter up with the sultan's royal vizier, Jafar.

Furious, Jasmine returns to the palace and confronts Jafar. He informs her that the urchin was executed for kidnapping the princess. Jasmine races from the room, heartbroken and in tears.

The savior she thought could become more is dead and it's all her fault.

Aladdin is very much alive and captive in the royal dungeon, after Jafar recognized him as 'the diamond in the rough' – the one person who can safely enter the Cave of Wonders to retrieve the magic lamp he desires.

Disheartened, Aladdin slumps against his cell wall. How could a princess ever love a 'street rat' like him? Jafar appears disguised as an old man, offering to lead Aladdin to treasures sufficient to win any princess's heart. They escape and, filled with new hope, Aladdin enters the Cave of Wonders with strict instructions to 'touch nothing but the lamp'. He finds the dusty old lamp, but before he passes it out to the old man, the cave collapses, leaving Jafar outside, lampless and angry.

Trapped with no way out, Aladdin examines the lamp, rubbing at a worn inscription. A large genie appears, offering Aladdin three wishes. Excited, Aladdin uses his street smarts to trick the genie into helping him escape on a magic carpet without using a wish. Once free, he contemplates what to wish for. Genie confesses, if given the chance, he'd wish for freedom from the lamp and Aladdin promises to use his third wish to do this. Then his mind turns to Jasmine. The genie can't make people fall in love, but he can transform them into a wealthy prince worthy of a princess. Finally Aladdin's dreams are within reach. He's no longer worthless or a street rat. He's someone who matters – a prince!

Prince Ali Ababwa and his procession enter the palace gates. The sultan is impressed. Jasmine, not so. She sees another rich, pompous prince, too full of himself and his wealth to be interesting, or interested in her as anything more than a prize. She tells him exactly what she thinks, then storms from the room.

Aladdin approaches Jasmine again on her bedroom balcony, only to be rebuffed. Again. Fed up, he steps over the side and onto the magic carpet. Jasmine is intrigued, and when Prince Ali reaches up and asks her if she trusts him in the same way as the street urchin, she warily takes his hand and steps onto the carpet.

They share a magical night, and under the moonlight Aladdin digs himself further into dishonesty, professing to be a prince who dresses as an urchin to escape the suffocation of royal life. Jasmine falls a little more under his spell, relating all too closely to his lies.

Head in the clouds, his goals and dreams finally within reach, Aladdin leaves Jasmine only to be seized by Jafar's guards. They tie him up and toss him into a lake, forcing him to use his second wish to escape. He returns to the palace to find Jafar hypnotizing the sultan into giving him Jasmine's hand in marriage. Aladdin breaks the spell and Jafar vanishes. Jasmine rushes into Aladdin's arms. Delighted and relieved his daughter has finally found love, the sultan gives them his blessing. Giddy with happiness, the couple head for the garden where Jasmine excitedly announces that once they are married Aladdin will be sultan and rule Agrabah.

Hit by feelings of inadequacy, Aladdin is torn. The finery, the lamp, the lies – none of it makes him a real prince worthy of a princess. Much as his conscience niggles, freeing Genie and telling Jasmine the truth is not an option – he won't risk losing everything he's come to love.

Then Jafar steals the lamp and Aladdin's worst fears become reality. Jafar transforms into a powerful sorcerer, snatching control of the kingdom, but not before he exposes Aladdin's deception. Desperate, Aladdin tries to explain, but Jafar magics him away, leaving Jasmine hurt and disillusioned and prey to the evil vizier's plans. Aladdin's guilt is overwhelming, but he won't give in. He must return to Agrabah and right the wrongs born of his deceit. That means returning as Aladdin, not Prince Ali.

Aladdin fights to save the kingdom and the woman he loves, despite knowing they can never be his. Finally, Jafar is defeated by his own greed, wishing to become an all-powerful genie. He is sucked into his lamp and banished to the Cave of Wonders. Jasmine runs to Aladdin and he apologizes for his deception. She can't help but forgive him. He's proved his love and strength of character by returning and saving both her and the kingdom. Plus, she loves him. Yet Agraban law says they can never be together.

Witnessing their love, Genie offers to use Aladdin's last wish to make him a prince again. Steadfast, Aladdin refuses – he'll no longer pretend to be something he's not. Fulfilling his promise, he wishes for Genie's freedom. Despite understanding, Jasmine is devastated. If not for that stupid law! Then the sultan proclaims a new law – a princess can marry anyone she chooses.

With a smile, Jasmine wraps Aladdin's hand in hers and chooses the man she loves.

There you have it – four different synopses, four different lengths, all establishing the different world, the central characters, the central theme, the major turning points, resolution and conclusion of Disney's *Aladdin*.

Take note of what I've included and what I left out.

This story contains a beautiful assortment of colorful and quirky characters. The monkey, Abu, who is Aladdin's constant companion. The tiger, Raja, Jasmine's 'pet' and friend. And of course, Jafar's parrot, Iago. Did I include any of these characters in the synopsis? No. Even the magic carpet made a very brief, cameo appearance. And only when required. As for the others, they are secondary characters, and while they are fun and cute, they aren't intrinsic to Aladdin and Jasmine's romance. They belong in your story, not your synopsis.

And what about the plot points? For those familiar with the movie, you'll notice I excluded quite a few. These include the entire sequence of events before Aladdin and Jasmine meet, starting with Jafar's journey to the Cave of Wonders. Even Aladdin's chase through the city with the royal guards didn't make a mention. These are both interesting and exciting incidents, but they don't add to the central characters' story or their romantic journey. And after all, we are talking about a romance here.

So, what can we take away from these examples? Make sure your story makes sense. That means only including plot points required for clarity or that feed directly into the journey of your central characters and their growing romance.

One example in Disney's *Aladdin* is the scene in which the Sands of Time identify Aladdin as the only one who can safely secure the lamp for Jafar. If not for this plot point, Jafar would have no reason to incarcerate Aladdin and lead him to the Cave of Wonders. There'd be no reason for him to urge Aladdin to enter the cave. Aladdin would never find the lamp or the genie, and his ability to circumvent his conflicts and achieve his goal – to become a prince and snag the princess's interest – would be greatly reduced. Hence, this plot point has earned its place in the synopsis.

Don't include secondary plot points or characters unless absolutely necessary. Notice I named Jafar in my synopsis, despite stating earlier that naming secondary characters is a no-no. In this case I made an executive decision to disregard my advice and it worked. My reasoning? As Aladdin's primary antagonist, Jafar features multiple times in multiple plot points; using his name made referencing him clearer, while less wordy and cumbersome, all objectives we're aiming for when crafting our synopsis.

There may be times you find yourself in a similar situation, and that's okay. Just ensure before you go ahead and contravene the rules that your reasoning is calculated and the resulting synopsis is enhanced. Make sure that the effect isn't long-winded, complicated or confusing, that the synopsis is better for the change, not worse.

Which leads to my next piece of advice: don't use long-winded or wordy sentence structure. Keep it direct. Keep it brief. Keep it simple. Do allow your unique voice and style to shine through. Do make it interesting, colorful reading. And above all, do have fun. I know the word 'fun' isn't usually synonymous with the synopsis, but the more you practice the *Simply Synopsis* method, the easier it will become.

Remember, if you enjoy writing your synopsis, your enjoyment will shine through and your audience will enjoy reading it. And their enjoyment will bring you one step closer to your end goal – snagging an agent or editor's interest and winning that much coveted publishing contract.

Your turn . . .

Now you've gained the tools and method for crafting a synopsis, why not have a go? Pick a well-known fairytale or movie and list the major turning points. Analyze the central characters and formulate their GMC. Write a logline or premise. Create a world-building statement. Then build a synopsis.

Then take a look at your current work in progress and do the same.

Perhaps your story is finished, or perhaps it's not. Perhaps your synopsis will assist you in identifying any plot holes or deficiencies in your characterization. Perhaps it'll help you break through a moment of writer's block or provide the ammunition to strengthen a character or scene and give it momentum and depth.

Perhaps it will win you that contract you've coveted since the moment you knew you wanted to write.

CHAPTER 12
IN SUMMARY

So, there it is, the *Simply Synopsis* strategy – a simple, methodical, logical method for crafting a synopsis.

Let's briefly run though the steps you've taken to get here:

1. Identify backstory events that feed directly into your central characters' GMCs. Add these sparingly to your orienting paragraphs or the body of your synopsis to give context to your central characters' GMCs, their actions, reactions and emotions.

2. Create the orienting paragraphs incorporating the following four key elements:
   » Hook
   » World-building
   » Central theme
   » Central characters

3. Identify major turning points and create turning point paragraphs by applying the six-step structure for major turning points. Make sure you cover all six steps:
   » Plot
   » Character
   » Action
   » Motivation
   » Reaction
   » Impact

4. Create the resolution and conclusion paragraphs by applying the six-step structure for major turning points.

5. Edit and refine your synopsis bearing in mind the following:
   » Voice
   » Tone
   » Secondary characters
   » Secondary plots
   » Explanations of central theme or message
   » Dialogue – do or don't?
   » Point of view
   » Rhetorical questions
   » Sectioning a synopsis – yes or no?
   » Brevity
   » Vocabulary
   » Evocative language
6. Format your synopsis as per submission guidelines.
7. Hit 'send'!

And there you have it. An overview of the steps toward building a truly superb synopsis.

I hope by the time you read this chapter, your standpoint on the synopsis has shifted. I hope the thought of summarizing your 100,000-plus word novel into a few pages isn't as daunting or as impossible as it seemed before you were introduced to the *Simply Synopsis* method. And more, I hope you take this very important message away with you:

Make your synopsis yours, just as you make your story yours. Use tone and voice to reflect your unique way of storytelling; use emotive language and active verbs to create tension and emotion; use an economy of words to maintain pace; and lastly, keep it simple.

Make your synopsis stand out and make it a winning tool in your journey to publication.

I wish you the best of luck!

ABOUT THE AUTHOR

Michelle Somers is a bookworm from way back. An ex-Kiwi who now calls Australia home, she's a professional killer and matchmaker, a storyteller and a romantic. Words are her power and her passion. Her heroes and heroines always get their happy ever after, but she'll put them through one hell of a journey to get there.

Michelle lives in Melbourne, Australia, with her real life hero and three little heroes in the making. And Emerald, a furry black feline who thinks she's a dog.

Her debut novel, *Lethal in Love* won the Romance Writers of Australia's 2016 Romantic Book of the Year (RuBY) and the 2013 Valerie Parv Award.

ACKNOWLEDGEMENTS

There are always a string of wonderful souls instrumental to the birth and cultivation of a book, and this book is no exception.

Simply Synopsis would not have been possible if not for the input from so many talented authors. I'd like to list and thank each one of them here:

Rachel Bailey	Kylie Griffin	Miranda Morgan
Anna Campbell	Lauren James	Bronwyn Parry
Anna Cowan	Clare Lucy	Valerie Parv
Anne Gracie	Ebony McKenna	

Thank you all for your support, words of wisdom and generosity in the making of this book. Its contents are all-the-more richer because of each of your contributions.

As always, thank you to the gorgeous women of Melbourne Romance Writers Guild (MRWG). Your love, encouragement and never ending faith have been the fuel to this wild ride that has become my writing journey. I love, admire and appreciate each and every one of you. And to Romance Writers of Australia (RWA), thank you for your camaraderie, support and generosity of knowledge since the moment I joined your ranks.

A big shout out to my fabulous cover designer, Lana Pecherczyk, for creating a sock-rocking cover, and my editor, Ruth Kennedy, for making my manuscript sparkle.

And as always, thank you to my wonderful boys, one big, three small, for your ever-growing love and encouragement. And your belief that I can do anything.

With your love, I know I can.

COMING IN 2018 . . .

SIMPLY CHARACTERS

A comprehensive guide to creating engaging,
multi-dimensional, believable characters.

Visit www.michelle-somers.com for more information.

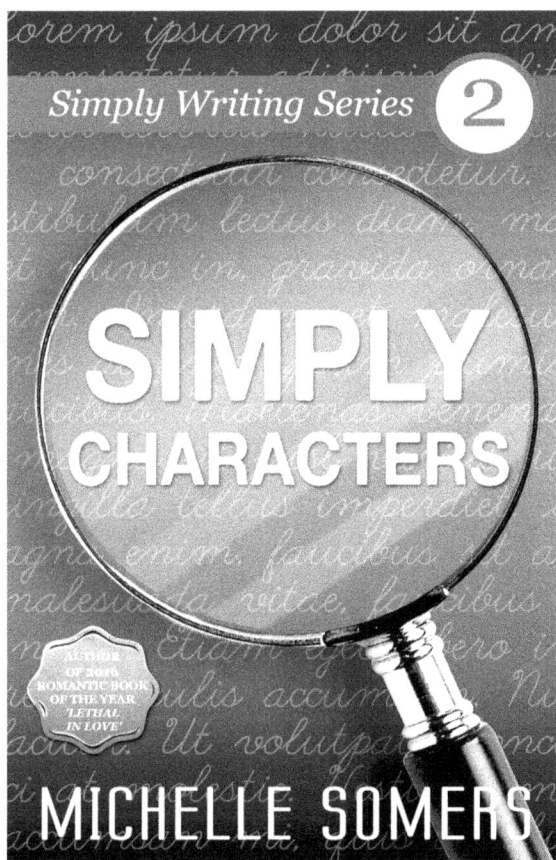

www.ingramcontent.com/pod-product-compliance
Lightning Source LLC
Chambersburg PA
CBHW072131020426
42334CB00018B/1752